THE BOOK OF UNKNOWING

FROM ENLIGHTENMENT TO EMBODIMENT

BY

FRED DAVIS

EDITED AND WITH AN INTRODUCTION BY

JOHN AMES

DEDICATION

THIS BOOK IS DEDICATED TO MY DEAR FRIENDS,

SHARON DESJARLAIS

AND

ROLAND JACKMAN

TOGETHER THEY LOVINGLY, MASTERFULLY,

AMAZINGLY

TURNED A LITTLE TEACHING INTO A BIG ONE.

Thank you.

I couldn't have done it without you.
Nor would I have wanted to.

I love you both.

ACKNOWLEDGEMENTS

I am deeply grateful to **John Ames**, without whom this book simply would not exist. John took my columns and made a book out of them. It's quite a transformation, and he has handled the whole project with consummate skill and an awake mind.

Once John had the book, he then penned the introduction. He's not actually printing it, but he did most everything else. For me, it's just like doing sessions with people: I don't do any of the work, yet I wind up with the money and the credit. Better to be lucky than good.

John taught English and film studies at Santa Fe College in Gainesville, Florida. John is the co-author of two books, and the author of two more, including a novel, *Adventures in Nowhere*. He is also an editor for AwakeningClarityNow.com, and I'm delighted to claim him as both my friend and close personal advisor.

John is not the kind of fellow who would be comfortable with my telling him that I love him, so let me say that I really like him a *lot*. He is a wise and cool guy.

Georgette Cressend, The Living Method's Events Manager, has unselfishly, and I should say *joyfully* been of tremendous assistance to this teaching in the last year. She makes it easy and pleasurable for a man who dislikes travel to leave home. Her spare bedroom is always open, as are her heart and mind and ear. All I have to do is show up.

Thank you, Georgette. I love you.

Georgette offers private sessions in the Asheville area, which has become my second home. She is wholly wonderful.

And last, yet nonetheless foremost, I want to thank my beautiful and totally remarkable wife, **Betsy Hackett-Davis**. Without her, *I* would not exist. Thank you, my love, for everything you do, and more importantly, for everything you *are*. Because of you (and Willy!) I find myself living a charmed life instead of a damned one.

1

TABLE OF CONTENTS

FOREWORD

Up until the day I first came across Fred Davis, I was jonesing to do one of those 10-day silent-meditation retreats. I'd talked to enough people who'd been through them to know it was going to be excruciating. Not the silence so much (although my friends howled at the thought of me keeping my mouth shut), but the endless hours of meditation.

Still, after nearly 30 years on the spiritual path, I was willing to take the pain if it would get me to the Holy Grail: Spiritual Awakening.

A year earlier I wouldn't have even been able to say that's was what I was searching for. I knew I'd worked my way from one end of the spiritual smorgasbord to the other looking for *something*. I'd chanted with Siddha Yogis and Nichiren Buddhists. I studied the Christian mystics and practiced Contemplative Prayer. I dove deep into the Course in Miracles and dabbled in the Kabbalah. I even converted to Catholicism in search of the Christ — a pretty extreme step for a Jew.

But awakening? I assumed that would take a few more lifetimes. And then only if I was lucky.

So imagine my surprise when I discovered there were people who were waking up right *now*. It first dawned on me when I read a book by Jan Frazier called *When Fear Falls Away*. She's a beautiful writer who, in the middle of a cancer scare, spontaneously woke up to her true nature. And she never felt another moment of fear.

I ate up each word like a luscious dessert. Then I wondered, do I have to get cancer to wake up? I hoped not, but still. Jan couldn't say how it happened to her. So she certainly couldn't guide me.

Once the doorway to the possibility of awakening had cracked open, however, it could not be shut. So I dove into the "direct path" of awakening. I listened to CDs by Adyashanti. Watched YouTube videos of Gangaji. And took classes from a whole host of beautiful non-duality teachers who could tell me all about awakening.

4

But it wasn't until I met this guy from South Carolina — Fred Davis — that I realized someone could actually walk you right through the door. In about 2 hours.

I gathered he was up to something different when I was reading his first book, *The Book of Undoing*. I was on a plane flying home to South Florida from Atlanta. And as the wheels hit the runway, everything shifted. And in an instant, I *got* it.

It's a cliché, I know. But the truth had been right there in front of me the entire time. I just couldn't access it until I had Fred guiding me, pointer by pointer. And if I could get all that from a book, I wondered, what would happen if I worked with him directly? So I did an Awakening session with Fred by Skype. And everything became even more clear.

Since then, with Fred's help, I continue to come back to a foundation of clarity. The bonus? Those ancient texts I studied all those years — from the Eastern sages to the Christian mystics to Jesus Christ himself — they all suddenly made sense.

So if you're satisfied being on the spiritual path, by all means, please continue. But if you're ready to find out what you've been on the path *for*, I urge you to read this book. Fred has a gift for using language in a way that cuts right through to the truth. And he does it with such hilarity, you can't help but want to read more.

I can honestly say that Fred Davis has been the most important milestone on my journey to waking up to our true nature. And I am honored to call him my teacher, my mentor and my friend.

Sharon Desjarlais

Co-Creator of ClientRich.com *and* ManifestationMysterySchool.com
Jupiter, Florida
April 30, 2014

PREFACE

Much to the amazement of my regular readers, I am going to keep this short.

With the exception of the biographical article, From Destitution to Deliverance, which was first printed in the online spiritual journal ONE: The Magazine, all of these articles first appeared on either my original website, Awakening Clarity, or the current AwakeningClarityNow.com. You will find some small bit of duplication of content; that is the way of columns, and not the way of books.

The Book of Unknowing picks up where The Book of Undoing left off. The Book of Undoing was about waking up, and this book is about what happens next.

Many of us thought that coming to know our True Nature was going to be the end of the spiritual road, that we would somehow "graduate". Those of us who've woken up now know better. Awakening is very often, but not always, the end of *seeking*, but it's the starting point for awakened living.

This is where the rubber meets the road. It's not "our" enlightenment, and it doesn't happen for "our" purposes. Awakening occurs and functions for its own purposes. We can choose to be good servants of Awakeness, by allowing it to take over, or we can choose to resist what's coming anyway, and be taken out like so many dodos and dinosaurs.

Allowing Conscious Awakeness to live through us without resistance is what spirituality is really all about. That's what saints and mystics have always known. They told us the truth, and they showed us a path, but we didn't want to hear it, or walk it.

We've been unconscious long enough. The planet is in deep trouble. Einstein said that "No problem can be solved from the same level of consciousness that created it." We are out of our league here. The more we try to fix things the worse things gets.

Enter the Natural State, the True State, where we see can see things as they really are. We're a mess, and so is our home, but we've got to come out of denial and *see* it. We need an "outside" intervention, and we're the only ones who can host it.

On this world, humans are the only units through which consciousness can come to know itself. We made the mess, and now we've got to clean it up and turn it around. The only problem is that we don't know how to do it. Essentially "channeling" the higher intelligence that *we are* is the only chance we've got.

The way to save our planet, or ourselves and our children, and oh yes, for those other organisms is to save ourselves first. Like a bunch of drunks with ugly hangovers, we've got to walk out of the bar and into the dawn and open our eyes to the morning after.

We have to wake up now folks. Lots and lots and lots of us. It's been a fun dream, and a good run, but one way or the other all of that is now coming to a close. Radical change is already happening. Our only options are to get behind it, or be run over by it.

There is just one thing going on, and we are It. When we're living in a state of conscious unity, the higher intelligence we host can and does *naturally* change our thinking and our behavior, *without* the negative polar effects science seems to be unable to avoid.

As we learn to witness our own unskillful patterns, and become open to being other than the way we are, patterns will shift. Nature will handle this through us if we'll let it. It's not yet too late, but it's damn close.

It appears that only a fresh state of being can save our world. We've got to step out of *becoming* and into Being. Awakeness is the answer. This is the age that the world completely changes, the time when it takes a radical shift unlike anything that's ever been seen, or even imagined.

We are the ones we've been waiting for. *Now* is the time. The answer to our problems lies inside, not outside. Let's get busy.

Fred Davis
Columbia, SC
May 5, 2014

INTRODUCTION

Fred Davis is something different in the nondual universe. When he pops up on your Skype screen for a session, he does not exude that vaguely melancholy perfume of personality that you find in some other teachers. Fred seems more like a man who fell into a vat of personality perfume and has not had time to dry off before calling you.

If you close your eyes, you can almost imagine that you have stumbled onto a rerun of *The Andy Griffith Show*, and if you are a sophisticate, you may be inclined to dismiss Fred in the same way *The Andy Griffith Show* was sometimes dismissed as a hayseed comedy rather than being recognized for the work of genius it was. So who is this fellow who has written the bursts of thought that make up this book, and presuming he is awake and can help you be the same, how did he get where he is?

To me, Fred looks like the remains of a southern good old boy, a type I have had the privilege of seeing around me for most of my life. The term good old boy, however, is tricky because for a lot of people, it summons the image of a heavyset drunk in the infield of a stock car race, hooting at the top of his lungs. And there is some truth in that. Good old boys come in all grades, but the high-grade version is a special and uniquely compelling arising.

The first thing you notice about a prime good old boy is his unbridled enthusiasm.
Wherever he is, he is involved and probably dominating the scene, not because he so much wants to dominate but because he has more energy and interest than anyone in the room. This can be taken for egomania, and that possibility cannot be discounted, but the good old boy's attitude goes beyond simple egoism. He does not want all the shine on himself—he wants you to shine too. I was riding in an airboat with a good old boy years ago, sitting and quietly enjoying the experience, as is my way. Jake looked over at me and yelled, "John! Stand up and get the full effect!" That is a good old boy all over. He wants you on board. Whatever is happening, he wants you to get the full effect.

Fred's first wife describes their initial date to a one-man stage show as follows: "Fred's laugh took on a life of its own. That laugh stood out. It rang out loud and ohhhhh so clear...a guffaw to be proud of! The only problem was that Fred appeared to 'get' a lot of jokes that no one else in the audience did. And not just one time. Oh no...it happened over and over...and over. The show was certainly witty, and there were lots of laughs, but when it was extra quiet and the crowd was rapt in attention...there was that lone, strong, resonating peal of Fred's laughter. I'm sure I elbowed him, but it didn't help. There I was, Ms. Don't Notice Me, sitting next to the loudest, most noticeable person in the entire theater...I cringe remembering how mortified I was!" Any introvert who has been around a good old boy can sympathize.

Laughter is a big thing with these guys. Sometimes, it is genuine because something strikes them as funny, but just as often, maybe more often, their laughter is an invitation to enjoyment. To us more constricted souls, it may seem forced. We prefer to laugh only when it's really funny, as if the act should be reserved for something pure. A good old boy laughs not just to reflect good feelings but to promote them. He believes he can lure a good time in if he uses the right bait. For him, life is a participation sport: otherwise, what's the point?

The good old boy is often a scamp. He recognizes that some people need rules, just not him. What rules he does recognize, he is inclined to bend, sometimes way out of shape, but he usually is not involved in crimes that directly hurt anyone. He is not likely to hit you over the head and take your wallet. He likes you too much for that. He prefers some form of game-like deviltry that involves a bit of competition, like outflanking the revenuers on a moonshine run. If he succeeds, then why not? If he gets caught, he is usually genial about it.

We know that Fred has been a scamp or worse. He has referred to some of it in his writings: "I was arrested in 2004 for having been a less-than-wonderful guy back in my drinking days. Some folks to whom I had delivered a real live, heart-felt apology decided that an apology simply wasn't good enough. They arranged to have a couple of policemen drop by my house early one sunny morning and cart me off to jail."

A good old boy's lust for life often leads him to drugs and alcohol, which like the ready laugh, are ways of intensifying the moment. And that is often a trap from which he finds it difficult to escape. He likes to fly high, and if he is not careful, he will forget how to do it unaided. At his best he will be judicious. A story is told locally of a good old boy in a nearby town who got roaring drunk once a year on his birthday. On that day, he was a pain in the ass. The rest of the year, he was a model citizen. Would that all good old boys were capable of that sort of restraint.

Fred wasn't. His drinking left him barefoot and homeless in a Portland, Oregon park: "Yes, I was living there in a park, in the bushes, scared and hungry, with blisters on my feet the size of the palm of your hand. ... I had sold my sleeping bag to buy a couple of bottles, and then I'd caught some kind of lung infection.

My voice sounded like rocks grinding against each other. I wished I would die, but I noticed I didn't. That's the funny thing about alcoholism; it kills you if and when it wants to, not when you want it to."

And this is another aspect of the good old boy's story. As much as he has a capacity for the enthusiastic embrace of life's joys, he has an equal capacity for suffering. In his exuberance, he may conclude that life is his paramour and will do all he commands. When he finds otherwise, the fall is disastrous. Most of us manage to paddle our way down stream without being sucked into a whirlpool. In doing so, we manage to cling to the illusion that we have some control in our lives. The good old boy, however, can fall from the height of supreme confidence to the chasm of impotence, and that is a sensation that can stoke the spiritual fires.

Quite often after such a fall, a good old boy finds himself, as it is sometimes put, "slain in the spirit." He may become an evangelist, but if he does, he is not one of those mealy-mouthed types. If you are sitting too quietly during the service, he will turn and shout, "Can I get an Amen!" As always, he wants you on board. He doesn't stop being a good old boy when he takes to the cloth. Most likely, he is the laying-on-of-hands type. He's been slain, so you should be slain, and he is just the one to facilitate it. That old confidence is back. He's riding high again.

And this brings us to the current Fred Davis phenomenon. Fred says that he first noticed his unusual talent when he was talking to a guy in his front yard, a man who had no spiritual aspirations and had most assuredly never heard the word "nondual." But Fred, recently awakened in a big way, would not let that keep him from talking about it. Whatever scouring out the awakening experience had done, that scouring had not dimmed the good-old-boy impulse to enthusiastically share his experience. And to Fred's surprise, the guy in the yard woke up. This happened with numerous other people and led Fred to start developing his Living Method of Awakening.

Fred takes little credit for what happened then or for anything that has followed. He states forcefully that whatever comes through him is a mystery. He refers to his body and mind as Fredness or "the unit." If overwork happens and his wife asks him if he feels okay, he is likely to say, "I'm doing fine, but I notice the unit's in trouble." Fredness might feel pride, promote himself, and otherwise function in the relative world, but as Fred explains, he is just the framework through which presence expresses itself. And that framework retains the useful qualities of a good old boy: charisma, energy, sociability, passion for life, a burning desire to make things happen, an equal confidence that he *can* make things happen, and the gall to think he can bring you on board.

Fred's writing reflects those qualities. This book is a compilation of posts from his website, most pounded out in a fever of inspiration, often at 3 a.m. As his editor, I go in at a decent hour and tidy up. There's not much to do. Fred is good off the bat, and he has an authentic voice that I don't tamper with. We may disagree on how many exclamation marks, capitals, and italics are enough, but even toned down, his work is bursting with good-old-boy verve.

Fred hammers away at his subject and is not afraid to go over the same material more than once; on the contrary, he relishes it. "Repetition is the mother of clarity" is one of his credos. Nor is Fred intimidated by the fact that Truth cannot be captured in words, only hinted at. He rolls up his sleeves and chops wood anyway, following the good-old-boy premise that if you build a fire, something's bound to get cooked.

In these pages, you will find Fred's energetic pointers directing readers toward the discovery of their true nature, most especially his "The Looking Glass: Language as Mirror," reprinted here because of the enthusiastic response it has received from people around the world who have experienced a shift in perception while reading it. As you would expect from a good old boy, Fred disdains the "nothing-to-do-no-one-to-do-it" philosophy that sometimes surfaces in nondual circles. In "What IS Self-Realization Anyway?" for example, he challenges readers not to wait for spiritual lightning to strike through grace but to do something to lure grace in. Don't just sit around hoping, use some bait!

This is just the sort of attitude to be expected from a man who has the temerity to offer to wake you up if you will spend two hours with him. Fred estimates that he has had some degree of success with nearly 90% of his clients, so a big part of his mission is to help people stay awake whether their initial seeing has come through him or by other means. His analysis can be found in "Two Reasons You're Not Awake Anymore," "Practicing to be You," and numerous others.

Be ready for straight talk. Fred will call you on your evasions because he has used them all at one time or another in his checkered past. Here is Fred describing his own once-upon-a-time attitude: "I wanted a nice, lazy, sort of blissful, awakened life—hopefully continuously orgasmic—where I wouldn't have to remain alert, for God's sake. I mean, I didn't want any sort of Awakeness where I had to be responsible; no siree! I wanted it all done for me— right now—just like I always wanted everything else. Hop to it, God!"

Among his most charming writings are Fred's takes on how being awake shows up in everyday life. In "Postcards from the Gone Road," Fred describes the ingenious non-plan through which he and his wife Betsy lost weight. In "When Suffering Comes calling," you will learn how a broken alarm clock taught Fred a lesson in acceptance. In "The Wren's Story," a nesting bird shows Fred a life lived in the moment. "A Day in the Life of Awakeness," shows how an awakened perspective suffuses a typical day in Fred's life. There are amusing and useful takes on several such topics.

Fred is fond of using snowfall to describe one aspect of awakening. According to Fred, snow just falls. It does not need to fall on any particular place or any particular thing. However, when it falls on a tree, the tree gives the snow form, just as awakening is given form when it falls on a human being. In Fred's case, it fell on a good old boy, and he has been slain in the nondual spirit. When you read his thoughts, you can't help but feel that he genuinely wants you on board.

John Ames
Gainesville, Florida
May, 2014

ONE

FROM DESTITUTION TO DELIVERANCE

I was right on the edge of death.

It was early autumn of 1998 when I found myself living in Mount Tabor City Park in Portland, Oregon. Yes, I was living there, in a park, in the bushes, scared and hungry, with blisters on my feet the size of the palm of your hand. When you're homeless, the police don't even want to arrest you. You're not worth the trouble. So they just nudge you along, keeping you moving, moving, always moving. Not on my beat, buddy.

I had sold my sleeping bag to buy a couple of bottles, and then I'd caught some kind of lung infection. My voice sounded like rocks grinding against each other. I wished I would die, but I noticed I didn't. That's the funny thing about alcoholism; it kills you if and when it wants to, not when you want it to. As the booze ran out and I began to have to face reality, I couldn't help but look back to a decade before.

In 1988 I had been living in the suburbs of Columbia, South Carolina. I owned an enormously successful comic, gaming, and science fiction shop. I had a great wife, a nice house, four nice cars, and according to my lawyer and accountant, a fine future ahead of me. All I had to do was not screw it up.

That's a difficult thing for a practicing alcoholic to avoid. I had not the first clue on how to handle success, because it wasn't anything I was particularly familiar with. I was a crazy man with money.

But let's drop back a little further. When I used to tell my story in public I got to where I told it backwards, just to make sure I kept both me and the audience awake. I guess I'm doing that here as well.

In 1982 I woke up—that's always what it felt like at the end of a long run of drunkenness and active insanity—to find myself getting bed and board in the G. Werber Bryan Psychiatric Hospital in Columbia. This was a place where the doors were locked, I wasn't issued a key, and I wasn't allowed to play with anything sharp. I did get all the crayons I wanted.

This was my second visit to the same institution. I'd been there a year before and hadn't learned a damn thing. I was not big on learning; I was big on repeating. I know now that it was all part of a vast pattern, but at that time I'm afraid I was unable to bring the "light of consciousness" to bear on my wanton lifestyle. This second time around, however, a voice went off in my head as I sat in the dayroom drawing with my crayons. From out of nowhere and clear as a bell it said, "You should study Zen."

It would not have been any more ridiculous if the voice had said, "You should grow horns," or "You should take a look at quantum physics." Here is what I knew about Buddhism:

I had been out to Boulder and visited Chogyam Trungpa's Naropa Institute, which is now a university. It certainly wasn't then. This was 1976, and it was a wonderful madhouse with lots of serious Buddhists, artists, chakra workers, Rolfers and all kinds of folks who were misbehaving just badly enough to make things really interesting. However, I certainly wasn't there for Buddhism and found it an annoying distraction to my chief task. I was a drunken, romantic poet, straight (in my mind) out of Jack Kerouac's *On the Road*, and I was hunting down Allen Ginsberg at the Jack Kerouac School of Disembodied Poetics. I found him, too, along with Peter Orlovsky, Gregory Corso, and a bunch of other Beats I'd read about. Heady stuff. Great for drinking stories.

I happily invaded a house that the university owned and rented out to students. They generously housed me and kindly fed me, and in return I drank all their wine (several gallon jugs of it that I found in the basement where I slept in the bed Corso had recently abandoned). On my first night there at a party at Ginsberg's, I met a lot of the characters who were in *On the Road*, and I thought I'd died and gone to heaven.

What I'm telling you is that here I was, in the very heart of a slowly awakening America, and I didn't want any of it. Allen wanted to talk about sitting practice, and I wanted to talk about Howl, his wildly controversial literary bombshell. Fortunately, all of us wanted to drink, so I fit right in for a day or two. It was in the Naropa house that I made my first acquaintance with meditation cushions. I thought they made fine drinking stools, and if you fell off of them, you didn't have far to fall, which was great.

This all took place about six years before I woke up in the psychiatric hospital and heard the voice in my head saying, "You should study Zen." Prior to that strange moment in the asylum, that time in Colorado had represented the sum total of my knowledge—and interest—in things Buddhist or awakened, and as I sat in Bryan Psychiatric, I was—guess what—homeless and penniless. I had just come out of the Arizona desert where I had also nearly died, which was the only reason I paid any attention to that voice at all. If I'd had any other idea, I'm sure I wouldn't be writing this today. But I didn't have any other idea. What I did have was a voice in my head that spoke clearly and authoritatively and had a suggestion. So, to my amazement, when I was loosed from the institution—after promising not to kill myself right away and thus cast aspersions on their care—I took my voice's suggestion.

This was the beginning of an off and on, up and down spiritual journey that was to last twenty-five years. Since there was no Zen in my town, I tried to join the Tibetans in my town, but I soon discovered I wasn't a joiner. If I wasn't going to be made Dalai Lama, I didn't need them, though they thankfully taught me how to meditate properly. Years later I tried to join the Zen crew in Portland, but once again, if there was no room for Fred Davis-Roshi, I just couldn't be bothered.

So I studied and practiced independently, diligently, even relentlessly (when I studied and practiced). Then I started making money and all that quickly went away. However, once I drank my way out of all the new money I'd made, I once again found the idea of spirituality appealing. It was a way for me to win. I thought if I could just get enlightened, hopefully with a bunch of followers (mostly women would be fine), then I could sort of feel like my waste of a fine slice of the American Dream had all been a clever plan. Of course my scheming was all just madness.

In Portland, in 1992, I had my first real glimpse of my true nature. Sadly, I was deep in my cups at the time, and ego simply lapped that up and christened me "special." Understand, I was a drunken car salesman, but I nonetheless shaved my head, started wearing all black, and ran my poor wife off for a while. I eventually became functional again—for a practicing alcoholic, mind you—but that single night of freedom haunted me and taunted me like Dickens' Christmas ghosts. I just couldn't let go of it. It gnawed and gnawed at me, but reality just couldn't quite get through the alcoholism and unveil itself again. Until it did, of course. But I'm getting ahead of myself again.

I eventuality got out of that park by powering my way through a couple of bureaucrats who were used to saying no to people who had better odds of recovery but less personal drive than I had. They told me to leave the crisis hospital, but I said no. I kept saying no until they had a homeless shelter come pick me up and take me to the bed I'd been told didn't exist. I bow to the city of Portland for their crisis, detox, shelter, and recovery programs. That saved my life, plain and simple. Thank you very much.

It took me another two years to get sober, but the park was my bottom. Not a week goes by that I don't mention it, and it's been almost fifteen years since I was there. For a while I went back and forth between Twelve Step recovery and drunkenness until I once again hit a very bleak spot, and the park rose up in my vision. I knew I couldn't go there again. I couldn't take that level of misery anymore. I knew I had to quit drinking, and I knew I couldn't do it myself. So I turned myself in to the recovery people, fully surrendered—to my alcoholism only—at long last.

I was one of those guys who jumps into recovery with both feet. I hit the ground running and I didn't stop moving for more than a decade. I got very involved in working the steps. I worked them poorly, as I see it now, but enthusiastically. I used to tell people that apparently God paid more attention to intent than she did form. I saw a lot of people do the steps perfectly who never got through them and ended up in the ditch again. More than anything on earth, I wanted to stay out of the ditch. Frankly, I didn't want to stop drinking. Not for a minute. But I wanted a life again, and I wanted to stay out of the park, and if surrendering to formal recovery was what it took for me to stay sober, so be it. I personally benefited from that moment of clarity and so did a ton of guys I worked with for the next eleven years. Getting sober was the smartest decision I never made. Call it grace. There's nothing else to call it.

I cut no corners. I would tell guys I worked with, "All I can do is tell you how I did it, and I did it the hard way; I did it their way." And that's the truth. I was cookie cutter recovery, straight out of the book. And it worked! I got sober, and my life began to stabilize. To this day, many years later, I've never regained really solid financial footing. I never made it a priority. I made getting and staying sober a priority for a while, and then I made stretching the bounds of my spiritual experience a priority, and there just wasn't time or opportunity for a whole lot else. I was 47 years old when I got sober, a guy with a heavily checkered past, so it made sense to make my demands minimal.

When I was 18 months sober I let myself read my first Zen book in a long time. It took about three minutes for me to see where I was headed: a nondual path of recovery. I learned to transfer Nondual teachings into recovery-speak so that no one would be offended. When I got to the rooms of recovery, all I wanted was to get sober. Now that I was sober, all I wanted was enlightenment. I went at it as relentlessly as I had gone after sobriety.

In 2002, I discovered Eckhart Tolle, and that changed everything. I read, listened, watched, and dreamed Eckhart Tolle for the next two years. And it's a damn good thing I did, because I was arrested in 2004 for having been a less-than-wonderful guy back in my drinking days. Some Ninth Step work, which is where we make amends for our wrongs, backfired on me. I spent the next two years in fear of prison as I waited for my trial. I didn't go to prison, but I did land in an ugly life situation, and I wanted to die. But my then-girlfriend, now-wife's business partner had shot himself in the head in 2002, and I had helped her clean up the detritus of his life and death. It was very ugly and took a real toll on her, so there was no way on earth I was going to commit unblessed suicide on her. She promised she would bless it if things didn't work out but asked me to please give life a chance. Reluctantly, I did.

So, I felt like I couldn't live, but I clearly couldn't die either. I was caught in a vise. I didn't see it coming, but this viceness is a perfect set-up for a spontaneous awakening, should one feel like making a visitation, so to speak. In September 2006, while sitting in my living room in total life delusion and misery, that "visitation" arrived for a second time, fourteen years after the first glimpse. This was more than a glimpse, a lot more. I came to know my true nature. In conventional spiritual language, I "woke up."

It was quite an awakening—it felt like it took the top of my head off. I moved from misery to bliss in the blink of an eye. Suddenly, I knew. I knew who I was, and I knew that everything was just fine, even the beat-up little human unit I'd thought myself to be but which I was now looking at from slightly behind and above. I saw clearly that "Fred" was just a story, just a label attached to an automated pattern. And since Fred was empty, so were all of his deep fears and dark concerns. It was all empty, every bit of it. When seen from awareness itself, all was well in the world, all was unimaginably fine in the world of dreams and drama.

Before I go any further here, let me say that what I am describing here is a spiritual experience. This experience was the sideshow, not the awakening. Experiences of this magnitude are fairly rare, I think, and if you don't have one you'll probably be better off. There is no intrinsic connection between this spiritual experience and enlightenment. As beautiful and profound as these experiences can be, they are very likely to serve chiefly as distractions. We get so caught up in the candy that accompanied the awakening that we overlook awakening itself.

Awakening can be very subtle, or very sharp, as it was in my case, or anywhere in between. Realization itself is not about visions, or an LSD-like experience, or feeling vast and blissful. That's the candy. It's great, and I'm all for a hot and spicy spiritual experience, but it is completely unnecessary. I've had dozens of people wake up while talking to me, and very few of them have had an explosive experience. Often there are tears and laughter, and once in a while there's a big bang, but just as often there is a simple "Oh." Or maybe an "Oh, wow." And this is sometimes followed by, "Oh my God!" It's a lot of fun to be a part of these awakenings; every one of them is different, and every one of them is wonderful.

Realization came, at least for me, in the way of an initial download, so to speak, followed by a series of downloads. I actually didn't get all that many direct answers, but the knowledge I did get caused nearly all of my questions to dissipate. Here's another example of that.

I once sat down to lunch with a woman I thought was a nearly hopeless case. From what she'd told me in the first few minutes of our meeting, I couldn't believe she wasn't even on the planet where awakening could happen. But she'd gone to a lot of trouble to meet with me, so with a heavy heart and all the enthusiasm I could muster, I gave her my absolute best shot.

An hour into our conversation she grabbed my hand and burst into tears. She just held my hand, looked up at me, and cried like a baby. She knew, and I knew she knew. "Welcome home," I told her as she cried across the table from me. She then proceeded to spend the next hour sounding like someone who'd been awake for years. Her whole use of language shifted as understanding dawned. She sounded like a spiritual teacher. Instantly. It was the most amazing, radical shift I'd ever seen.

17

In my own case, after that second awakening, insight followed insight as I came to see more and more over the course of several days. When we discover that we are the vastness, the awake space that is already everywhere, and already awake, it is startling. It's always a surprise. During this same time period, however, ego was doing a rapid rebuild. Yes, it happens. In fact, in my experience as a teacher, it almost always happens. And then the brightness begins to fade. I found myself no longer operating from present realization, but from the memory of a former realization. This is the well-trodden path, but I didn't know it at the time. We call this phenomenon "oscillation."

Yet despite a lot of back-and-forth oscillation for a few years, I never could truly unsee what I'd seen; although the "overwhelming" quality of the realization has now, thankfully, gone away. Now, everything is just sort of steady. Take it from me, steady is much, much better than the bliss candy that often accompanies an awakening. You don't need it, and you're probably better off if you don't get it. A nice, quiet "aha!" is much easier to deal with, and a good deal less distracting.

I went through the cycling of "I-got-it, I-lost-it" for 3 1/2 years, until the spring of 2010, when I spent 45 minutes on the phone one evening with Scott Kiloby. He easily pulled me out of that unsteady state, and into stability with some simple inquiry. Later he helped me orient within this brighter awakeness through continued pointers and dialoguing. I learned that lesson well. It's what I do for others now. I've come full circle.

So I had reached steady-ness, but I still wasn't really clear. In the same way that I invaded the Naropa house in Boulder, I invaded Greg Goode's email account. I'd read his book *Standing as Awareness* and was completely blown away by it. He was a friend of Scott's, so I introduced myself, and then regularly hijacked his attention for the next year or so. What a gentleman! I hounded him with countless emails, always presenting my highest view only to have him dismiss it without dismissing me. That's an art, and he's got it in spades.

I also spent a year or so in online satsangs with Rupert Spira. There was just a small group of us early on, so that I could really engage Rupert in a one-on-one, very meaningful and illuminating way. There just aren't a whole lot of people who are clearer than the folks who so kindly helped me. It would have been cruel to unload this much insanity and arrogance on just one man, so I'm glad the universe mercifully did it the way it did. When I started the website *Awakening Clarity* in the summer of 2011, I left the recovery world, because I knew I could no longer serve two masters. Insofar as the website goes, I had no idea what I was doing. But one of the things I had unknowingly done was open up a way for me to write out my junk. I freely aired my ongoing awakening, along with my missteps and my arrogance. It was great; I recommend it.

I also soon found myself addressing a growing worldwide audience, which really made me think and test whatever I put down. "Do you really know this for yourself?" And "Is it really true for you?" were the two questions I constantly entertained. They are great questions to ask yourself as you go along. Forget answers. Go for questions. It's inquiry that frees us.

If we don't impede it, spiritual awaking is an organic thing, ever-changing as we become clearer and clearer. The goal is not to transcend relativity, but to embrace it. I am not exclusively this little man who's typing this, but I am that little man. I am not exclusively the vastness, but I am also the vastness. I am both. I am the whole thing, the one thing—this thing. And you can say the same. Everyone can, whether they are clear, or cloudy.

Today, I write about Nonduality and I teach via Skype, or through my website, or wherever. Who could guess or dream of such a turnabout? From a destitute guy dying in the bushes of a city park to having the opportunity to facilitate and counsel people all over the world? It's almost inconceivable. You have to ask yourself, What were the odds this would happen? One hundred percent. It had to happen because it happened. There is no alternative to what is, no parallel universes where woulda-coulda-shoulda rule. There is just This. THIS that is right here, right now, and This is enough.

I can't write any more without launching into self-promotion. That's something this unit does, and I have to keep an eye on it. Back in my days in recovery, some people would talk about being too nervous to tell their drunkalogue-and-redemption story in a public meeting of their peers. The only thing that ever made me nervous was the idea that somebody might get to the microphone before I did. This unit is a ham. It's apt to misbehave.

So I'll end here . . .

TWO

THE LIVING METHOD: WAKING UP SUDDENLY, CLEARING UP SLOWLY

The models left to us by the great spiritual traditions are at core strikingly similar. We start in the dark and advance through egoic ignorance and dogmatic immaturity as we slowly move toward the elusive yet intoxicating goal of true knowledge and mature understanding. It's rather like climbing a set of stairs. All traditions agree that the foot of the stairs is a place of suffering and misidentification. And they agree that a seeker must start up the steps, though each tradition describes the steps upward and the landing toward which they lead differently.

As we begin to climb the stairs, we all hope (even suspect!) that we are going to be the spiritual lottery winner. No seeker ever takes a pilgrimage under the assumption they will fail. What I notice, however, is that most pilgrims die on the steps, somewhere in their journey from the awfully muddy *Here* at the bottom of the steps, where the truth supposedly isn't, to the glistening *There* at the top, where the truth supposedly is. Only a remarkably small percentage of adherents of any tradition I'm aware of, including Nonduality, ever actually "make it to the top," and wake up. The numbers of seekers may be large, but the percentage who succeed is alarmingly small. This dreary fact is known and ignored by seekers everywhere. The common pattern is to do your practices, occasionally beat yourself up because you don't seem to be getting anywhere, and then go back and start again, but those damn stairs are so steep!

I was a seeker for almost a quarter of a century. That, my friends, is a long time. Now, here's the sad part. If I mentally go back to the very first teacher I had, I can remember one night when she and I had a discussion, and she told me the truth. That was in 1983. I had my first large awakening in 2006. Why the twenty-three years of seeking after I had heard the truth? My teacher had done her job those many years before, but I couldn't do mine. And therein lies the rub. I couldn't hear her. Jesus said, "He who hath ears, let him hear." I had no ears in 1983. None of us do—until we do. So the truth goes unrecognized until it doesn't. So that's the way things have always been, but is it the way it has to be from here on?

No.

When I woke up, I discovered that despite my years of study and practice, the only thing I was missing was the only thing that counts: experiential knowledge of our true nature. Study and practices are good things. I'm not pooh-poohing them. All of the context that came before my awakening was finally quite useful. The veil dropped further and faster because of it. The years devoted to independent Zen study, and zazen practice, had not been wasted. Neither was the tedious inquiry which I really didn't understand how to do.
Yet no amount of study or meditation; no ritual or chant, no bell or gong led me directly into realization. And it never would have. Because it can't, not directly. It may prepare the mind and perhaps even the body to some degree, but where all of that stuff becomes most useful is in the post-awakening clearing process. In the end, it was my awful, can't-live-like this/can't-not-live-like-this life story that really did the job.

I call that place of hopelessness The Vise of Suffering, where spontaneous surrender arises. And it works when it works. It worked to get me sober, and then six years later it worked to wake me up. The Vise of Suffering has surely caused more awakenings than any other factor. Yet The Vise is not a sure thing by any means. It doesn't work all the time. It doesn't even work most of the time. It only works when it works, and there's no way to predict it or to court it. Fortunately it's not necessary to do so.

I have had hundreds of people wake up while they were talking to me either in person, on the phone, or the largest percentage, on Skype. How can this happen when the traditions almost all emphasize that long agonizing climb up the stairs with its heartrending tedium and uncertainty? How did I get into a position to facilitate so many awakenings?
It started even before my own awakening. Years ago, long before I woke up, when I was sober but still crazy as a bedbug, I told my then-girlfriend-now-wife, "Betsy, it's all about patterns. If I ever wake up and see the truth, I know it'll be all about patterns." When my big moment came, I found I was right.

The incredible dream we call day-to-day reality is not only all about patterns, it is in itself a sort of meta-pattern. No need to go into all of that here. But the part I didn't know back then, which I most certainly do know now, is that we can unwind the dream's hypnotic hold in just a couple of hours by consciously weaving and utilizing another pattern, a living template.

Enter The Living Method of Awakening. Once I realized that I had some kind of loose method of helping people wake up, I started out to test it. What evolved was a pattern of questioning which is rather like the offspring of some mad coupling between Eastern philosophy and the Socratic Method.

What do I mean when I say "method"?

There is a pattern to my teaching. Think of it as a template with hard edges that holds something alive, something that flows in its own way, without need of thought, direction, or correction. I start in the same place in every Awakening Session, yet not even the first five minutes of an Awakening Session is universal. The client will respond to the initial inquiry in their unique, snow-flake way, and the living, flowing, interior of the template will move on its own to meet them right where they are.

Clients may tense up in fear, but the pattern will immediately move to meet that and relax them. The client's ego may begin to rise and challenge, but the pattern will quickly, sometimes even sharply, move in to send it back down the rabbit hole. Clients may get lost in their story, but the pattern moves to efficiently redirect and reestablish cooperative flow.

The facilitator, Fred Davis, does none of this; it just happens. If they're going to work, these sessions have to move quickly and smoothly—there's no time for personal involvement. We don't challenge one thing in these sessions, we challenge everything. The mind becomes disoriented. Long-held assumptions are seen through. Lifetime beliefs collapse. Basically the client is seeded with doubt and then clobbered with it. Relentless repetition helps this new seeing be driven deep into the client's mind.

I've had people compare The Living Method to Ramana's work and to Douglas Harding's, yet it's really not like either. With me, if a client wants to wake up more than they want to keep dreaming, they'll wake up when they talk to me. Every time. The Living Method works right out of the gate on about 90% of the people I talk to, even the toughest cases. Ironically, those tough cases are often the people who know most about Nondualism. They give all the right sounding answers but just can't let go. It's hard on them, and it's hard on me.

In a way, though, all my clients are tough. If they weren't tough cases, they wouldn't be sitting in front of me. They've already tried a lot of paths before they try The Living Method. Fred Davis does not have the cachet of an Eckhart Tolle, Adyashanti, or Byron Katie. Fred who?

My house, so to speak, is generally the last house on the block. Most people call me when they've run out of options. They can't really believe that I can do what I say I can—I wouldn't have been able to believe it either, I get that completely—but they want so badly to believe that The Blessed Event maybe, just maybe, could happen for them, so they call, often against their better judgment.

Most are smart people. The profession that accounts for the largest percentage of my client base is the mental health profession, whether it be clinicians, researchers, or educators. I spend a lot of time with the Three P's: psychiatrists, psychologists, and professors. But they come from all professions: physicians, lawyers, mathematicians, professional life coaches, high-flying entrepreneurs, and lots of just regular folks like me. I've worked with people in their 20's and people in their 80's. As to gender, it's about a 50-50 split between the sexes.

I have worked with people from all of the great traditions, as well as a lot of people from no tradition at all. Some of my clients have been on the spiritual path—dedicated people, mind you—for ten, twenty, thirty, even forty years without finding out who

they really are. With The Living Method, they wake up in two hours. Over and over again.
Why is this important? Because this is the only teaching I know of that starts with enlightenment. We don't start you at the bottom of the stairs with The Living Method, we start you at the top, at the landing.

Once you're awake, which is the norm with this method, and you actually see things the way they are, then we point you down the stairs, allowing you to gain context and experience that deepens and broadens your awakening. Clarity and stability can take a long time. But why not spend that time sharpening your true seeing instead of trying to get to true seeing? This is the opening that never ends. When you change where you're looking from, what you're looking at changes.

Is this it? The ultimate answer? I don't think there's just one "it," but this is certainly an incredibly valuable resource for those who are ready for it, and it's absolutely flexible, and thus capable of working in league with the other spiritual resources. It's new, it's fast, and it's incredibly effective. It's worth a look.

Why die on the steps?

THREE

SOLVING THE AWAKENING PUZZLE

I'm very big on saying things like "The easiest way to wake up is to notice that you're already awake." Strange as it may seem, that's a fundamental truth, but it's not always helpful. I was on the enlightenment trail for a long time, decades, before I recognized my own always already awake condition, and I can well remember when such a comment was nothing short of maddening. Let's take a closer look at what the statement points to and see if we can find something that will be helpful, no matter where you appear to be in your journey.

Back in the day, my responses to hearing "You're already awake" caused me all kinds of suffering. I got angry and asked myself, "Why in the hell would they tell me something so absurd as that?" I got my feelings hurt because I felt as if people were somehow making fun my dreadful awakelessness. I felt stupid that I couldn't see something so many said was obvious, and I mentally accused anyone making that statement of being a liar or fool. Any of these reactions is a fair response for an ego because the pronouncement "You're already awake" does on the surface seem like a ridiculous statement, but while I was busily registering anger and confusion, I was too caught up to ask, "Who are these teachers talking to when they say this?" The answer to this question is the key to solving the awakening puzzle.

We think self-realization is all about us, and that's just not the way things work. Back when I suffered over being told I was already awake, I believed there was a "me" housed in my body. I thought this me controlled what I was thinking and doing, so I naturally deduced that my thoughts and deeds must play a direct role in getting me through the Gateless Gate. How wrong I was.

I believed then, as so many do, that awakening occurs to the well-intentioned, good, wise, humble, and dedicated, but my own experience of awakening shows that it can also come to the poorly intentioned, hollow, stupid, arrogant, and erratic, such as myself. Awakeness does what it does for its own reasons, and it plays no favorites. Thank goodness!

In 1982, when the thought "You should study Zen" first popped into my head, it was clearly directed at the human unit that was spending its afternoon drawing with crayons in the day room of a locked ward in a mental institution. It was directed toward me, meaning Fred, if you'll pardon the expression. And it was a damned reasonable suggestion, given that the very same Fred unit had been in the very same room almost exactly one year before and had apparently not learned enough between visits to keep itself out of that room.

So far so good.

The problem arose when I presumed that since the thought to study Zen had arisen in my head, that it was being presented for my approval and benefit, the "my" in this case meaning my ego. I saw it as a self-help type of suggestion by some higher functioning part of me or perhaps by some unknown mystical entity, but wherever it came from, I thought it was being made available for the physical survival, mental comfort, and spiritual advancement of Fred. Nothing could have been further from the truth. Although I considered myself to be both brilliant and astute—a real comer, so to speak—in the harsh light of day, anyone other than myself could see that I could neither feed nor house myself, or hang onto a job, relationship, or anything else of consequence. It was about all I could do to stay out of jail—most of the time.

The total absence of any evidence to support my lofty self-image did not keep me from holding it. This is called denial. It went hand in hand with the fierce denial of the core cause of my hospitalization: addiction. I was, in essence, addicted to everything that had ever felt good. Chief among them were alcohol and compulsive gambling. Mix those two with chain smoking, and maybe a helpful amphetamine or two, and man oh man, you've really got something! I was a mess.

When I got out of the hospital, I discovered a Brand New Story. Now I could be Fred the Mystic. I would be able to dress up my clamoring desires in spiritual clothing, and hail my newly found superiority over the unwashed masses from an entirely new position! Enlightenment (or almost as important, having people believe I was enlightened) looked to be just the vehicle for a guy with my checkered past to catch a ride on. Through Enlightenment, I would rise meteorically from the dead to compete again, and this time wear the crown of the winner I thought myself to be. To heck with big money. With Advanced Spirituality, I could now look down on the wealth that I did not have but still secretly craved. I also imagined that women would find my hot Zen self devastatingly sexy as well, which was a second big plus. Maybe I could even find a rich patron. Ah, the possibilities! I repeat: I was a mess.

25

Every motive I had was wrong. I was a very sick guy. Yet from the absolute position, none of this mattered one iota. Flow was positioning the Fred unit—that body, that Fredness pattern that we call Fred—right where it wanted it to be: onto the spiritual path. Flow didn't give a tinker's damn about what that unit's mind was thinking. Flow knows a harmless crank when it hears one. It's listening to 7,000,000,000 of them bemoan their conditions every day, so ignoring the unit I found special was all in a day's work.

After I did some reading, I confess that even I, the dedicated fraud and hedonist, caught the flavor of something that sounded very alluring. Suddenly I really did want to wake up. A quite sizable part of me still wanted to wake up for the aforementioned shallow and selfish reasons, but a new spark got struck while I was investigating just what in the heck this realization thing might really be. Of course I had no clue whatsoever as to its true nature. No one ever does, but that didn't stop the arising of a longing for it. We always want what we don't have—until we wake up. Then we want to keep that so badly that we chase it away by grasping for it.

First and foremost, enlightenment sounded like a way out. Most people on the spiritual path are looking for some variation of the same thing. They want out of suffering, out of their present life situation, out of delusion, out of the dream, or perhaps just out of the insane seeking cycle they find themselves caught in. I hear there are people who are moving toward something with their seeking rather than away from something, who are willfully and valiantly moving toward truth for the pure sake of truth, but I wasn't one of them, and they must be exceedingly rare, because I've yet to meet one. Everybody I talk to wants out of suffering, just like I did.

In the end, from the absolute view, personal motivations simply don't matter. All of that is simply story, just the window dressing flow creates, probably to lower the unit's resistance to doing what it's already fated to do anyway: take the spiritual journey. Flow loves efficiency but is equally happy to do things the hard way if it has to, even if that way may prove rather devastating to an individual unit. Whichever way it goes, we become, in essence, victims of grace. If our intention has been such that we are willing victims, then things will go more quickly, smoothly and comfortably for the unit involved, but they are going to go the way they go, and they will not long be turned, or ever be stopped.

I want to make it clear that I am not suggesting this is any kind of decision-making process by some sort of divine entity. No, no, no. I'm just reporting on the mechanism. My mind, any mind, is completely incapable of grasping how this all happens. I'm just saying that it does happen. I don't need to understand electricity to report on what a light switch does. Same thing here.

In my case, flow started out with a unit that had zero genuine interest in spirituality and had nothing even resembling humility, integrity, honesty, or tenacity. Yet flow began, with what we might call infinite patience (and it's hard not to attribute some measure of hilarity as well) to bring the unit's rebellious mind into alliance with its already compliant body. It began the process of waking me down, out of my head, and down into my body, which had always been fine because it is incapable of registering an opinion. Flow is what drives a petunia through a crack in the sidewalk, impels a bat to grow larger ears, and waits out a red sun that is collapsing over the period of a billion years, so dealing with something no more complicated than an idiot is no real challenge.

The first time around, I was full-on into spirituality for about eighteen months. Then I fell into a promising business opportunity and dropped sainthood like a hot rock. I moved in and out of spirituality for the next few years—mostly out—because a human can completely abandon itself to only a single master at a time, and I had an old one made new again: money. I made enough of that over the next few years to help me come to believe that I was altogether bulletproof, so I started drinking and gambling again. In fairly short order I cleverly drank and gambled my way right out of prosperity and back into my default position of poverty. When I hit bottom from that dive, guess what suddenly looked appealing again? That's right, Zen and the enlightenment card. Does this begin to look like a pattern to you? It does to me, too. Humans are all about patterns, whether they work or they don't work.

So, I made my second big foray into the world of Spirit. I was not gently moved onto the spiritual path the second time around anymore than I was the first. In fact, in my entire spiritual history, I was never quietly or softly positioned, because without the presence of a desperate hair-on-fire crisis, it was impossible for me to be open to any idea beyond my own puny thoughts. Subtlety didn't work with me. So in my case, "positioning" was more like being thrown from a speeding airliner without a parachute. Each time I briefly struggled futilely, and I each time I landed with a loud splat.

During that next foray into Zen I went the full course, at least for a solo adventurer. I meditated a lot. I read constantly. I discovered self-inquiry and drove myself absolutely crazy with it. Amazingly enough, half of the time I was actually sincere. And by golly, I got a glimpse of my true nature; I surely did. Yet hot on the heels of that cosmic seeing, even before the glow had passed, I returned to caretaking my addictions, and I stayed at that task for another nine years. Oh, I had been permanently imprinted by that first amazing glimpse, trust me on that, but I still had a lot of seeking to do, which is what my addictions were: seeking mechanisms. It was still all about Fredness.

Notice, however, that regardless of the unit's addictions or its beliefs, opinions, and positions, BOPs, I call them, it had nonetheless been positioned to acquire a hell of a lot of context. Context is absolutely invaluable once we awaken. I liken it to snow falling on a tree instead of bare ground. The snow doesn't need the tree, but because of that context it can have a much richer experience of itself.

So, in early 2000, as the fragile charade of my life began to crack again, I once again found myself attracted to my old fallback, compulsive spirituality. I got sober, I moved back into practicing Zen, and discovered Eckhart Tolle, which led to other nondual authors. Then I started another business. If I was still a betting man—which I most certainly am not—I would bet you dimes to donuts that I would have dumped spirituality again within a month of starting that business because I suddenly had another option. Whenever I had a promising option, spirituality always came in second, meaning last.

But flow was running out of patience. In Twelve Step recovery they tell you that you have to make your amends for all the things you've done wrong, but they don't say anything about them having to be accepted. Some folks to whom I had delivered a real live, heart-felt apology decided that an apology simply wasn't good enough. They arranged to have a couple of policemen drop by my house early one sunny morning and cart me off to jail.

Boy, did that spiritual thing ever look good again! Perhaps I could do both the new business—which I would need to flog for legal fees—and simultaneously pursue spirituality? Did people actually live like that? Two balls in the air at the same time? Who knew? Previously I couldn't have found the word "balance" in a dictionary. Now I was being forced into some semblance of it, because without money I couldn't support or defend myself, and without spirituality I would have gone over-the-top, never-get-out, locked-ward crazy-crazy.

For two and a half years, from the day of my arrest until the day of my hearing, I ate, drank, and slept spiritual teachings, all the while pumping up my fledgling business. I listened to Eckhart's soothing baritone twelve to sixteen hours a day for months: upstairs, downstairs, and in my car. I needed that calm overlay to keep the voice in my head from driving me nuts. After my trial, where I properly pled guilty, I went into total despair. The terms of my sentence struck a terrible financial blow to my already modest lifestyle and greatly restricted my physical freedom. And of course there was that nagging little element called humiliation. Six weeks after the trial, in a dark hole of depression, wanting to die, but forced by a loving promise to continue living, on one bright morning while sitting in my living room, I came to recognize my true nature.

Funny how that works.

Flow had done its job. Despite this unit's errant path and aberrant thinking, an ugly duckling had been miraculously turned into a swan; a lotus had risen from the mud. I confess that though I had tried and tried to storm the Gateless Gate, I never really thought it would actually happen. And prior to the moment of that awakening, I wasn't even confident that there was such a thing as awakening. I'd been a hopeful faker, so maybe everybody else was, too. Our personal worlds have precious little to do with facts. They are built entirely of our personalized beliefs, opinions, and positions—BOPs.

So, what about solving the awakening puzzle can be learned from my story? You probably thought I'd never get there. First, when teachers say, "You are already awake," they aren't talking about "little you," in my case Fredness. They are talking about "Big You." Little you is not only not awake, it is incapable of being awake. The lights are on, but nobody's home. The one who wants to wake up will never wake up. Fredness is still asleep. My ego never woke up, and neither will yours. That's why I say awakening happened *through* me rather than *to* me. It is, in fact, Livingness itself that wakes up. It wakes up from the dream that it is a single unit exclusively, and sees that it contains all units of all kinds universally. There is nothing that is not you. You are every grain of sand, every thought anyone ever had about a grain of sand, and everything that man or nature ever built with a grain of sand. All arisings, including the one reading this sentence right now, rise and fall within you, Big You. You, Big You, indeed, are awake. Always have been, always will be, can't not be. There's no need to wake you up, and no way to wake you up since you're already awake.

28

So is there anything that Little You can do? Apparently, yes, and that brings us to the second lesson that can be gleaned from my history. Whether you are one of those humble well-intentioned seekers or a rogue like I was, you can gain context through Little You. All the while Fredness was conniving, lying to himself, and going back on his resolutions, he was at least gaining context. When the moment came, Fredness provided a framework for awakening. That makes a big difference.

All I can hope to do is to help you point back at that which is doing the pointing, and help you come to recognize your own, infinite, eternal, true nature. The puzzle is never solved; rather, it drops away after you, Big You, sees that it was never there to begin with.

Awakening is not about these units you're wearing, as a tree wears snow. They can appear to impede or advance spiritual progress, just as Fredness did for so many years. But whence come the directions to cooperate or hinder? Those, too, come from Livingness, can't not come from Livingness, because Livingness is all there is, and you—Big You—are It.

FOUR

THE LARGE, THE SMALL, THE SUBTLE AND THE PROFOUND

I've had the privilege of witnessing hundreds of people wake up, and I am here to tell you that awakening comes in every flavor, size, shape, and color, While at core it is the same thing, how its apparent arrival is experienced, and how deep or stable it is varies broadly. I've had people almost explode in front of me, like a bolt of lightning had hit them. I've seen others go into hysterics of laughing or fits of uncontrollable weeping. There are folks who go back and forth between the two. And sometimes they just say, "Oh." or "You're kidding."

There is tremendous variation. Interestingly, the unit's initial reaction is not in any way a tip-off as to what the overall effect of their awakening will be. Another way to put it is that the size of the spiritual experience which often accompanies awakening is not in any way a reliable indicator of how long the experiencer will be clear or stable.

I have seen clients who had brilliant awakenings—large, profound events—develop a sense of oscillation within a few hours or days. (I say a sense of oscillation, because clearly there can't be any real oscillation). Where is oneness going to go when it "oscillates"? Can oneness move? Can oneness somehow go outside of itself, and then move back into itself?

On the other hand, I've had people with low-key reactions achieve relative stability almost immediately. They might just grin and say something like, "I'll be doggoned; it was here all along wasn't it?" Some of these subtler event folks are today remarkably stable and clear.

I've also seen people wake up but be back in the dream before the end of the session. Crazy as it sounds, we have to be willing not only to awaken but also to accept awakening over and over again, and some people simply are not that willing. I wasn't ready to wake up for 23 years, and it took me several more years to entirely accept it in an ongoing way, so who am I to point a finger?

However, once we see What Is clearly, it is also seen that there are no alternatives to What Is. That's what makes everything so simple in the enlightened view: What we think about What Is doesn't count. We don't actually get a vote. We try to cast our make-believe vote anyway, but it changes absolutely nothing other than the unit's state. The unit gets to suffer all it wants until it doesn't want to suffer any longer, which is usually about the time we are feeling forced into continued seeking. We're sick of that, too, but we notice we can't stop.

We continue to seek whether we like it or not because we don't get a vote! IT's doing what IT's doing, and that includes what IT's doing with us! Whatever else Nature might be, I promise you that it is not a democracy! And even if we think we are members of the party that is out of office, somewhere outside of oneness, we're not. There's only oneness, and we're part of it!

My mantra for arisings is "This too, this too." Mind is always looking for the exception—the arising that it can resist without penalty. There isn't one. Accept or suffer; those are the only two choices. Thus I say, "This too, this too."

Awakening is simply a grand dose of truth. It's fabulous, life-changing, and all of that, but essentially it's just a seeing of the truth, seeing things as they really are. When this wave of truth comes rolling in toward shore, it crashes upon a unit. After the crash, It continues to come through a lump of raw conditioning for so long as that body-mind lives.

Our overall receptivity, that mysterious combination of willingness, tenacity, and earnestness, which is usually directly proportional to the depth and stability of conscious awareness that we experience during and after awakening, depends more on the body-mind than it does on our teacher, our tradition, or other outside circumstances. You may be at a spiritual retreat or crossing Times Square, dieting or ordering pizza, helping the poor or gambling away your last cent, but those circumstances are less important in your awakeness than the state of your body-mind, your unit.

Is this unit ripe? Has it suffered enough? Is it tired enough? Is it at enough of a dead end to confess the truth? Is it ready to be open and honest? Does it want to wake up badly enough? Is it willing?

We can't make it be if it's not. (Although we can certainly create fertile ground!) We can't make it not be if it is. Even if we can answer "Yes" to awakening, there are a hundred different degrees of it, And those degrees are what tell the tale. Thus the small-event awakening may be incredibly deep and profound, clear and stable, while a large-event awakening may fall to pieces in fairly short order, And then come back!

Awakening happens the way it happens, and our determination to control it will always be what's stopping it. Who is it that wants to control it? That's what we always miss. Forget what's going on around you, who is it that isn't happy with it? There's the key to awakening, right there.

Do you imagine Awakeness cares about how or when the unit wants to wake up? It does not. It's happy with whatever shows up. Always, Which only leaves ego to care about all that stuff, Which only leaves ego available to suffer, because—you guessed it—ego doesn't get a vote.

We don't control the dream, whether we're asleep or awake, No one does. Nothing does. It's all just happening, spontaneously unrolling and unfolding into this What Is that is not other than us. We wake up to the dream, but not from the dream.

A dream unit is sitting at a dream desk writing an article about the dream from within the dream. We could say that this particular unit, however, is a window. There's a great deal less Fredness here than there used to be. Due to the reduction of Fredness, the light of Truth from beyond the dream can now shine through that window into the dream. And relativity, the very thing many of us were hoping to transcend, is now experienced more beautifully, and lived more skillfully.

This is the miracle. This is what enlightenment is actually all about—abidance and embodiment. But we can't really start on that journey until we first wake up to our True Nature. Once we know who we are, not from hearsay, but from our own direct experience, then we find ourselves, then we begin the real journey toward clarity, and this is the journey that never ends.

FIVE

SO AM I AWAKE YET OR WHAT?

If you're concerned about whether you're awake or not, then you're not—at least not right now.

Such a question would not occur to conscious Awakeness. Since we've already said that everyone is equally awake, then all we are ever talking about is whether or not we are consciously awake, knowingly awake. If we can get clear on this, we can see that there's no room left for higher or lower, better or worse, more spiritual or less. All of those qualities spring from positions, which conscious awareness doesn't have. The apparently separate being that awareness is working through will certainly have positions, but the Awakeness behind it will not. So if you are asking whether or not you are awake, you're not.

But even in this understanding, there is a potential trap. A couple of weeks ago, I told a wise friend that I was going to write this article, and he immediately shot me the following terrific advice: "It's a good idea, but there is one important caveat that needs to be included. One should watch out for that desire [to be awake] going underground and manifesting as a certainty and confidence that I am awake. 'Before, I was in doubt. Fred said that this doubt is a sign that I am not awake. Therefore I have seen through this and no longer have the question.'"

Do you see how tricky all of this is? You can hardly dance for stepping on your own feet! The point is that you can't kid yourself. You just have to keep sticking your chin out until it doesn't occur to you to stick it out anymore.

So maybe you still want to know if you're awake or not. We can come at the question another way, by asking a series of counter questions: "Who's this you who's claiming to be awake? Who is this you that can't seem to stay awake? Who woke up to begin with?" Gotcha.

I say that because when we have an authentic seeing, or more accurately when authentic being arises openly, the one common factor, regardless of background, is that the one who appears to be experiencing this dramatic unveiling is now known to be utterly nonexistent, at least in terms of autonomy. From the standpoint of the mind, it's a real head shaker. You just can't figure it out, and you can't keep from trying. However, from the absolute view, there's nothing to figure out. It's just the way things are.

From the point of initial seeing on, the seeking game changes. We're no longer trying to move ahead into clarity. We're done with all that nonsense, for goodness sake. Now, by God, we're trying to move back into clarity! This form of seeking is even more fruitless and deadly than what we were doing before, because we usually have more openness and humility before such an event than we do afterwards! We didn't know what we didn't know. Now we think we do. It's stagnating. So how does all of this happen?

More often than not, this freshly exposed, non-existent self quickly appropriates this new awakening information, adds it to its wealth of treasures that are designed to keep it special and separate, and then plows right on as deluded as ever, even though it knows better. So far as I know, there's no chance of actually unseeing what's been seen. There's no unringing that bell. Yet side-by-side with that knowing there can and usually does exist a denial of and a resistance to that very same knowing. To know *That* is to lose *me*, which is a damn tough call until it's not. Thus we have the paradox from hell that runs until it doesn't. As close to the truth as words will allow is to say that the hoax itself perpetuates the hoax. Sometimes this hoaxness even goes on to teach other people that they can be autonomous non-existent beings too! Who said spirituality was pretty?

I've made embarrassing proclamations and ugly errors in deed and word; I've too often unwittingly tortured those around me. In short, I've repeatedly made an ass out of myself: "Hi, Bill. have you noticed that I'm basically the new, improved Ramana Maharshi? No? Well, it probably doesn't show up for someone like you just yet. Others see it, I mean at least probably they do. They should. At the very least, I see it! Once you get a little clearer—if you ever do—you'll easily be able to spot it, too! In the meantime, hang on my every word, okay?" For humor's sake, I've made this example far-fetched, but sadly enough, it's not as far-fetched as I'd like it to be.

Still want to know if you're awake? Let's talk about language for a moment. By listing all those "Who's this you?" questions a couple of paragraphs ago, I'm not advocating staying away from personal pronouns; that's tiresome and ridiculous. We can and do still use language provisionally. I love language, hence the writerness. We can actually use words just the same as we did prior to an experience of seeing-being, but with the tacit understanding that these words are inherently untrue. So, why am I unlikely to treat "Am I awake or not?" as a simple case of using words in a provisional sense? Maybe the question is being asked by someone who is actually awake. Not likely. The nature and context of the question will cause me to sense an underlying cloudiness in the questioner. It just shows. The reason I can see it is not because I'm some sort of Cool Nondual. I can see it because I've ignorantly bloodied my nose in exactly that same way against exactly the same mirror—over and over again. For years.

Let me go on to suggest that if we find ourselves "tip-toeing through the language fields," afraid to say "I need an aspirin" or "I need to go to the bathroom," then we might want to check ourselves to make sure that this careful tip-toeing is not a cover-up for our own unsureness or a move to impress others with the implied proclamation, "Look at me! I am enlightened! There's NO ONE here, I say!"

I know all about this. I'm guilty of having performed entire ballets of such figurative tip-toeing. So what? It's common and it's okay; it's all part of the charade and there's no shame in it. Yet the death of spiritual progress lies in believing these positions and remaining caught in them. It's easier than you want to think. I'm lucky to have someone who'll shove me out of them before I even know I'm in them. I guarantee you he'll find parts of this very article to clobber me with. It's great! Believing our own positions, including the sweet lie that we have no positions, happens most often when we are going it alone, as I did for a long, long time. I didn't want help from anyone who might tell me I wasn't already awake! Which means I was caught in an endless loop. I was going to my own ego for outside advice. And then taking it! Oops.

Any decent teacher—and there are a lot of them out there—will easily point out our errors, help us remedy them by showing us the flaws in our thinking, and then sending us back to the path of direct experience. They help us climb down out of our heads and plant our feet back onto terra firma. I'm confident we can even catch this thing on our own if we're both willing and capable of being absolutely honest with ourselves. That's no easy trick. I couldn't do it, but if you can, my hat is off and I wish you well.

Still asking the question, "Am I awake or what?" Let's talk about profound misidentification. Say we have what appears to be a real seeing "event." We know in our hearts it's authentic. If it's real, there's never any doubt at the time. Suddenly we are grokking things we've never understood before. Books that were thick muck are now joyful reading and mysterious things our teachers have said are now understood. I've often laughed when such a thing bubbles up from long ago, and I see, "Damn, he/she was sharing obvious truth way back then." We have really and truly "seen the monkey" as I sometimes put it. We get it. Everything is swell. Until it's not.

The apparent seeing event may last a few seconds or a few days, but however long it lasts, at some point we begin to notice that it's wearing thin. Rather than living via experiencing, we're back caught in thought. We're now referencing our former experiencing through memory. We're back to living in interpretation instead of reality, and that is the place where we are likely to ask "Am I awake yet or what?"

By the way, it's common for doubts about an awakening-type experience to arise later. Did that really happen? Maybe they're right, and I *am* crazy! We sometimes deny the truth as surely as Jesus' disciples did in the Garden of Gethsemane. Oh well, we're only human. Aren't we?

The cruel truth is that our blissful event, like any event, passes, leaving us stranded as ordinary people in an ordinary world. What a drag! We liked the specialness better! However, conscious awareness is perfectly content with the extraordinary ordinary. Every story is seen to be equally unique and equally empty. In my opinion, which is not particularly humble, any seeing that runs contrary to this is not coming from Awakeness.

But knowing that the story is empty doesn't mean we adopt the absolute view as some code for living life at the relative level. The absolute view doesn't work for that. It'll just make you cold as hell and stupid as stone. We don't want to tell a friend whose mate just died that it's all hunky-dory because in truth their loved one was never with us in the first place. That's not wisdom, that's cruelty. Following an apparent seeing event, the attempt to transfer absolute-level views to the relative level or relative-level views to the absolute level is a key cause of confusion. And pain. They just don't mix. That's why they call all of this a paradox.

The question of whether or not we're awake is really not all that confusing. The truth is simple: when we're not functioning from Awakeness, we simply don't want to see that we're not. That's what happens with me, even now. I never fluctuate mentally any more. I know who I am 100% of the time—including when I'm not acting from who I am. There is no mental oscillation; thus, there is no longer any classic seeking. But I don't know who I am 100% of the time on the deepest gut level. Sometimes Fredness is 100% here, and sometimes Fredness is 100% not here. But there's never any 50/50 proposition, unless Fredness is 100% here, but is lying to itself and declaring that it's not. As a result, there is still subtle seeking.

There, I've said it. Shoot me. There is still some false sense of containership here, "within which" it feels like consciousness is functioning. Sometimes. Many of my negative behavior patterns are at last falling into line with my understanding, but I still reach for a book, click on Google News, do a chore "ahead of time," or work on my website to break mundane boredom and keep the mind rolling...toward a future that simply doesn't exist. That boredom notion tells the tale. There is no mundane boredom in conscious awareness because there is no mundane to be found.

I'm willing to be who I am, which includes accepting who I have been at every step in this amazing life, whether on a seemingly pious spiritual path or a decidedly wicked one. Only from this place of honesty, candor and surrender is Who I Really Am likely to come out of hiding and consciously, knowingly, stay out of hiding. I recommend the same approach to you as you attempt to answer the question, "So, am I awake yet or what?"

SIX

THE MOST IMPORTANT QUALITY FOR FULLY AWAKENING

Sony M., a writer who lives in the foothills of the Himalayas, wrote me the other day asking if I'd like to be included in his book, *The Big Book of Living Gurus: Satsang with 108 Spiritual Teachers from Around the World.* I told him sure and sent him the required materials. One of the things he asked for was my single most memorable Q&A with a student. I'm printing here what I sent him.

Q: What is the most important quality for a seeker to have in order to really wake up—to move into abiding, embodied Awakeness?

A: Without a doubt it's earnestness. That's what Nisargadatta said, and I'm in complete agreement with him.

Regardless of what shows up in the absolute view on the "other side" of a so-called awakening event regarding "all that nonsense" about individuals and effort, I notice that most of the time, most of the people who come to know their true nature do so after a long, earnest attempt to do it. There are exceptions to that rule, but this teaching works with the Law of Large Numbers, not the exceptions.

Even if we begin our spiritual journey from what looks like egoic intent—and I don't know anyone who didn't start from that—do we have the continuing humility, willingness, and fortitude to keep going, to keep asking questions in the face of the countless, ready answers we find in the spiritual marketplace? Are we willing to ask over and over and over again, "Is this true? Is this true for me?" in the face of so many attractive, tantalizing answers? We want so badly to belong, and we barely begin the journey before we want it to be over.

We come to spirituality in order to answer our questions, but we move into authentic spirituality when we begin to question our answers.

Once there has been an initial awakening, the standard movement is to breathe a sigh of relief that all the "seeking and stuff" is finally over. That was my initial reaction, and it's a fair one. But we don't then get to rest. Seeking may be over but awakening is not! Not hardly. We graduate seeking via the awakening event only to enter the new school of the awakening process.

Or we don't. We may simply decide to rest on our laurels instead. Think twice. There is no resting on our laurels. We are moving forward, or we are moving backward, but we are always moving. Resting may be comfortable, but it is the death of clarity.

Scores of people have woken up while they were talking with me, or shortly thereafter. Far fewer have continued to move from that place on toward abiding, embodied Awakeness. While we as individuals can never completely unsee what's been seen by Awakeness, we can totally forget its keen and highly relevant significance in regard to the plight of our planet and its suffering. By doing so we relegate our awakening to nothing more than a cool experience I had for me, and which I would very much like to have again. Or perhaps we purposefully cross it off our *Life List of Things to See and Do*, and move onto climbing Everest, jumping from an airplane, or reading the Greek classics in sequential order. Many will do exactly that, in fact.

My recommendation for the earnest seeker—and awakening cannot be denied to an earnest seeker—is that upon awakening you catch your breath and then immediately take the next step. Opening never ends unless we end it.

SEVEN

A FINGER POINTING AT THE MOON SPIRITUAL EXPERIENCE AS HAZARD

I've noticed something important in working with clients. There is a strong commonality between the people who seem to have the most trouble coming to an initial experience of the Understanding and those who "got it" but are on the pendulum swinging between clarity and cloudiness. The problem often lies in our expectations.

First, let's talk about what a spiritual experience is. We can say that it's a non-ordinary event that comes dressed in what we might call spiritual clothing: energy, light, visions, auditory messages, something like that. There is probably an aha! moment in which we suddenly see or understand something we did not previously understand, or we understand it in a different way. It is generally pleasurable, in some cases the most pleasurable event that a human can experience.

Few if any experiences will incorporate all of these facets, but they will include one or more. Sometimes, we can have a little "pop" of recognition, and that, too, is actually a spiritual experience, but we tend to downplay such things and relegate them to the shelf labeled "insights." Insights do not approach the coolness status reserved for spiritual experiences precisely because they lack the element of glamour. We want glamour. We want that experience to come in loud, wide open, absolutely clear, and employ about the same subtle tactics as a pair of gunmen in a home invasion. With that experience, we are forced to see/be the truth, so to speak.

And one other thing spiritual experiences is that we can report who it happened to: us. Spiritual experiences, even the best of them, still happen to an "I." If they didn't, we couldn't report them. In the absence of a sense of "I-ness," events cannot be recorded or reported. They can happen without any "I-ness," but only "I-ness" can record or report. The I-witness may be impersonal, and it may be way back in the background, but it's there.

These are the bones of a large and profound spiritual experience. We can report when it began, we can report when it ended, and we can even graph it, but it's clear that we had zero control over it. No need for us to "be present," when we are made to be, and that easy road seems to be the one we want to be driven down—all day every day.

I've had people tell me, "I don't care about a big awakening, I would be happy with just a little one!" This is actually a negotiating position they've adopted in lieu of getting what they want. It's like a gambler having moved from making the big score to just getting his money back. They don't know it when they tell me this, but it's not the truth. They're certainly telling me the truth as they know it, but it's not the truth.

I will share my experience with you: it's all I've got, so I might as well. It's limited, but it's not insignificant. In the last couple of years, I've had the good fortune to be present when a fair number of people got their first good, knowing look at their true nature. I've seen them "pop," as it's sometimes called, in person and on Skype, and I've heard them pop over the phone. In other cases, There's been a delayed pop that I've found out about later, often in an excited email.

Now, when I first started teaching, I thought that having someone awaken, however briefly, in any of the ways I just described would be rare. Instead, I find it's rather common. I don't mean ordinary when I say "common." I simply mean non-rare. No one could be more surprised at these non-rare occurrences than I am. For a while it completely shocked me. Today it delights me, but it doesn't shock.

What I am providing is "The Glimpse," an event that brings us face to face with our true nature. This glimpse is widely thought to be the starting point for deeper spirituality, and in the beginning, I thought that perhaps these awakenings would prove to be permanent, or that many of them would be. I was quite wrong there. I quickly found out that spiritual seekers are like other addicts such as overeaters and smokers: the quitting ain't so hard, but the staying quit is a bitch.

Seekers are addicted to their thoughts, and they simply cannot stand not taking them seriously for any length of time. I have been totally stunned to speak with people who've been awake in my presence, but who later cannot even recall it. I understand not being able to recall what it was that they "knew," Oscillating between"I got it" and "I lost it." But I was totally unprepared for people who cannot remember at all what they cried over and thanked me for. I was unprepared because I had conveniently forgotten that I did this as well. I not only forgot it: I denied it! The whole phenomenon is damn amazing, let me tell you. Man oh man, what a dream it is! My hat is off; there is nothing maya cannot do, except be real.

So, if The Glimpse isn't as difficult as it's been made out to be, and you haven't had one, the question has got to be WHY? Or, if you've had what you knew to be The

Glimpse at some time in the past, but that's not your present experience, and you can't seem to conjure up another one, the question again has got to be WHY?

Our nondual Shakespearean chorus will now chime in to tell us that "there's never an answer to a 'why' question." As always, the chorus is right, but again as always, they're only right from the absolute perspective. Just for the moment let's pretend there is an answer. My answer may not be the only answer, but the following, I promise, ranks high among The Apparent Causes of Apparent Long-term Separation.

The people I have had the least success with are people who think just like I used to think! I suspect that like attracts like in this case. These folks have a preset notion of what true reality should look like for them, and they have a fixed idea of how that seeing should arrive. This was my predicament for a long, long time. Grace eventually engineered an override for me, but I wouldn't bank on that happening for you, and I wouldn't wait to try something different.

What reality "should look like" to these folks is inevitably something other than *this*. And that thing-looking-other-than-this "should arrive" with a bang and holler that looks exactly like a classic, in-the-books, big-time spiritual experience, even if what they say is "I don't care about a big awakening, I would be happy with just a little one!" It's not the truth, because everybody who gets a glimpse immediately wants another one, and it "should be" both bigger and permanent. That's the mechanism.

The only problem with this approach is that it's generally fatal to acquiring the Understanding. If we insist on holding to this, then in the absence of grace, there'll be no more glimpses glimpsed, whether it's a first-time or a next-time. But depending on Grace is likely not as effective as cultivating an attitude that you might, just might, have some control over. What might that be?

It is often said "The ignorant reject what they see and believe what they think. The wise believe what they see and reject what they think." There it is, folks. If you're having trouble getting your glimpse or keeping it, this is almost surely why. We read a crystal clear truth like this, which is totally open and above board, and then we scratch our heads and go looking for the hidden meaning.

Only there is no hidden meaning. Our eyes are telling us, "Here, we are, look around. This is it: this here, right here, right now." Simultaneously our minds are telling us, "This can't be it." And therein lies the rub. There is a disconnect between what our eyes are telling us and what our minds are telling us, so we are faced with a choice as to which we are going to accept as truth. We typically opt for what our mind is saying, and I'm suggesting that this is not the the proper foundation on which to base further spiritual inquiry.

This strategic choice that will form the basis for fruitful spiritual inquiry is straightforward: do we operate from sure ego or confused awareness? We tend to go with the sureness, and we tend to be WRONG. Nonduality is not about answers, it's about questions.

I am far, far better off to accept this ancient observation as sound advice, and elect to throw my lot in with the wise, however confused I may be. By making that choice, I admit that I am not searching for something new to happen, I am simply washing the window through which I peer at the world. Sometimes I tell my clients: "These sessions are simply to keep the glass clear; they're not about making anything happen." When we change the way we look at things, the things we look at change, and the easiest way to change how we're looking at things is to change from where we're looking at them.

If we've not had a glimpse, it might be more important to investigate our secret expectations—or demands—before we go look at what that fresh material on Amazon or YouTube may have to offer us. It's fine to go to Amazon or YouTube, but go as Awareness open to something forgotten, not a seeker in search of something new. I've had more than one person turn directly away from awakening because reality didn't meet their expectations. Honest to goodness, I'm telling you the truth. Sometimes reality doesn't begin to knock us off our feet until we've spent a little time with it. That doesn't seem like the way things "should be," but it's nonetheless the way things are.

In a similar vein, if we have had a previous spiritual experience and think we are not now awake, then we have confused the delivery system with the payload. The bells and whistles have pulled our attention away from the fact that what was shown to us was that we'd always already been awake, could not, in fact, NOT be awake, that there's just one thing going on: the seeker is the sought, and anything in opposition to that is pure invention, utter fiction. We have once again invented the problem of separation, and now we are holding out for the fiction of our deliverance!

Standing as Awareness, however cloudy we may feel, cuts the legs out from underneath our story of future. What reality is going to look like, and how it's going to arrive—first time or "next" time—are both versions of that future story, which is a sure block to our path. It's absurd and completely human. It's what we do.

Until we don't.

EIGHT

LETTING GO OF OUR OLD SPIRITUAL IDEAS

It's not particularly unusual for me to stop a session and have a have a heart-to-heart talk with my client. People who have been around spirituality a long time often think they know a lot about enlightenment: what it really is, how it should show up for them, what that experience will be like, and what it'll be like for them afterward.

We don't have a clue.

Heck, I get it—I thought I knew all of these things, too. I had endless fantasies about enlightenment, but none of them was right. During my twenty-four years of seeking, my assumptions were wrong, completely wrong, and these old ideas and expectations did not function to free me: they worked to cage me.

I've personally never worked with anyone who turned out to be right about any of these things. That includes the many people who've had previous awakening experiences, but who are nonetheless not awake to this present arising. Counting ourselves as the exception to all the rules that apply to everyone else is a great way to stay outside the Gateless Gate.

Sometimes we get into an egoic contest with the very person who's trying to help us, and inquiry turns into argument. When this happens, we are far, far better off if we catch ourselves in the act of screwing ourselves and have a private "Come-to-Jesus" moment. So here's some advance notice on how to avoid resisting awakening.

What awakening calls for are three things I learned a lot about when I was in recovery: Honesty, Openness, and Willingness. The H.O.W. of the Twelve Steps is also the H.O.W. of awakening. I am not saying that the spiritual awakening typically found in Twelve Step recovery is the same as the spiritual awakening found in Nonduality. In all but the rarest of cases, it most certainly is not. But I am saying that the most successful approach is the same for both types.

HONESTY

Can we tell ourselves the truth? Can we admit that what we've been doing up to now isn't working? Will we concede that what we think, know, and believe has so far not brought us to awakening? If it hasn't worked for forty years., is it likely to do so today? Admit failure.

Can we confess that we don't actually know anything at all about awakening? Can we admit that we don't know what it really is, how it should show up for us, or what it will be like either when we awaken or after? Admit ignorance.

Have we noticed that our brain has failed us? Actually, we've failed our brain. We've asked it to do something that's impossible. We've asked it to figure out how reality works. It can't. It would if it could, but it can't. The part can't contain the whole. Admit limitation.

Have we noticed that whatever path we've been on has brought us here, wherever here is? Perhaps the path itself is trying to tell you something? Admit where we are.

OPENNESS

Can we leave our old ideas behind, like a snake sheds its skin, and be like a new person coming to a new thing? Suzuki-Roshi called this "Beginner's Mind." This is the mind we want to cultivate. Old Mind is what we want to empty as best we can. Can we come to the fountain with an empty cup so that something new can pour into it?

WILLINGNESS

Once the door is open, are we willing to actually walk through it? Are we willing to allow awakening to show up on its own terms? Are we willing to accept it when it does? Is our loyalty devoted to our old ideas that we love, to our dear teacher that we love, to our chosen sacred path that we love, or is it to ourselves? We have to decide. We have to be willing to accept awakening as it comes, when it comes. This is huge.

They call it The Gateless Gate, but the gate is not the only thing missing. In order to pass through the Gateless Gate, your luggage has to be missing. You can't bring a steamer trunk of old ideas with you. You can't even bring a change purse.

NINE

WHAT *IS* SELF-REALIZATION, ANYWAY?

Self-Realization has always been an open secret, There are excellent signposts pointing toward it and trails leading to it all over the world. They have been there for millennia. The problem is that these signposts and trails only become clear as signposts and trails in hindsight. Unless we are actually abiding within awakening, we will inevitably mistake the path for the destination. Given enough time and enough agreement, the path becomes a religion. Given less time and/or agreement, and it will be labeled a cult. The difference is chiefly measured in staying power and fervor, not in relative proximity to truth. There is no such thing as proximity to truth.

Nowadays, the world contains seemingly endless reams of tempting information on the topic of Self-Realization. Chiefly because of the Internet, knowledge about Self-Realization is easily available, but that knowledge is not so easily put to constructive use. To discover knowledge is not the equivalent of acquiring it. If I mucked around long enough in a diamond mine in South Africa, I could surely discover a fine gem. But I couldn't say that I had acquired it simply because I had found it. The authorities would never let me leave with it. My reach would exceed my grasp in the case of the diamond, and in the case of Self-Realization, reach exceeds grasp by about a million miles more, because if we think of Self-Realization as that diamond, even if I actually sneaked it away from the mine, I might look in my pocket a mile down the road only to find that it had disappeared. This is not to say it wouldn't still be in my pocket; on the contrary, I just wouldn't be unable to see, experience, or utilize it. That's the way it is with Self-Realization. It is as tantalizing as that diamond, and equally hard to find and keep.

So how do we finally grasp this diamond?

Pointer number one is that Self-Realization is essentially verbness. It's happening, or it's not, and it's happening right here, right now, or it's not happening at all. Self-Realization is like eating: it happens in the moment. Imagining or remembering a good meal may prove to be fascinating entertainment, but neither is a substitute for the real thing.

You may see yourself as standing at the edge of an abyss. On your side, there is a lot of noise about Self-Realization. You read about it, think about it, ask questions about it. Sometimes you think maybe you've got it, but then you think maybe you don't. From where you stand, Self-Realization seems impossible-to-comprehend and you feel that somewhere across that abyss is the real thing, the Self-Realization of which you can be certain. You feel you must cross that gap, but the necessary leap cannot be forcibly initiated by the subject. We must, for lack of a better word, call upon the phenomenon of "grace." Self-Realization cannot be figured out. It cannot be taught or bought. Historically speaking, it is only "fallen into" in the very rarest of cases. Having an awake teacher can help immeasurably, but absolutely nothing guarantees that a teacher can transmit Self-Realization, even to the most fervent student.

The good news is that grace can, in essence, be cultivated. To be struck by lightning is generally thought to be simply monumental bad luck. But tote a long metal pole around a golf course in the middle of a thunder storm, and one could be said to be courting it, even cultivating it. Nothing insures it, but your odds of being struck go way up. If you want to cultivate grace, do your practices. Sing, chant, pray, dance. Carry that metal pole until lightning strikes. You may just be struck sane.

Self-Realization pointer number two is that after Self-Realization has struck the first time we have to encourage it to continue striking, always in the Now, through our ongoing expression of willingness. I hate it for you, but I'm talking about spiritual practices again. Unless you are one of the very few who get purified by the first strike, you have to keep at it. Spiritual practices aren't necessary unless they are, but IF they are, then they ARE.

Until they're not.

It might seem beneath the dignity or wisdom of one who has glimpsed Truth to go back to humdrum meditation or some other practice, but that wise and dignified view of yourself shows that you need more practice. Once you are stable in your understanding, you can do as you like.

Pointer number three is to be willing to admit to yourself that you're not "realized" if you're not currently realizing. You'll never in a million years find what you think you already have. If you have to wonder, or you have to ask, then it's not happening. Again, go back to your practices or do anything you think will help, but don't pretend
.

Pointer number four covers all stages of the search for Self-Realization: Approach realization as if it is real. If you haven't had it, if you have oscillated out of it, or if you have had just a subtle glimpse, you might find yourself getting cynical, but cynicism is poisonous. It doesn't lead anywhere. Doubt is fine, even healthy, because you can stay open through doubt, but cynicism kills openness.

What diamond might these pointers help you find?

Here in a nutshell is what is being realized when the universe is realizing:There is just One. This is the central truth. It is the ramifications of this apparently simple, central, living truth that are staggering to both intellect and ego.

If there is just One, guess what there isn't? Two. There is only Not-two. So there's not an independent you. There's no Fred, no Tammy, no Charlie. There is certainly Fredness, Tammyness, and Charlieness: there are certainly memories and patterns and opinions and all that, but they are unmistakably seen to be running by themselves. There is not actually anyone home. It's all just happening. Everything is rising and falling spontaneously with the all-accepting spaciousness that is You.

In the absence of a "me," of a "center," of a "reference point," everything is seen to be just as it is. It's not good or bad; it's not big or little; it's not fast or slow. It just is. It can be said to be perfect, because there's no not-perfect, but even this "perfect" description is a layering on. There is only What Is, beyond judgment, beyond description, simply beyond. And yet it's right here.

The word "persona" comes from the Greek word for mask. God is wearing a whole bunch of masks and the "you" that you-think-you-are is one of them. As I once heard Adyashanti tell a questioner, "Don't misunderstand me. I'm not saying you don't have free will. I'm saying you don't exist." He means that there is no such thing as an individual. There's no separation in the universe, no division whatsoever. There is no center, and no circumference; no beginning and no end. There's just One Thing. We can call it God, or we can call it Lucy: It doesn't care. But YOU ARE IT, and I can say the same, as can the daffodil and the locust. There is just One True Story: I Am. (There is still a little storyness built in there, but that's for another day.)

One has to be willing to relinquish "me-ness" in order to embrace This Reality, which is why, regardless of the wide availability of these nondual teachings today, their following will NEVER be large. Who the hell wants to relinquish me-ness? No one, until they cannot do otherwise. This "otherwise" is why this teaching will always be passionate, regardless of size. Truth builds a fire within the dream-character that all the dream oceans in all the dream worlds cannot drown out.

So let's tell the truth: few are willing to make the required apparent sacrifice for more than a moment. That's fine. Have a party. Go talk about that moment and how great it was, and how you can't wait until you have another one. Listen to the stories from others about THEIR special moments. No problem. Build a better, more special dream-character and have a more spectacular dream life. There's no reason you shouldn't. But please, let's not call it spirituality. Let's call a spade a spade, as Chogyam Trungpa did many years ago. That's spiritual materialism. That's the diamond you will most likely find in your pocket, but don't mistake it for the real one.

47

I hope I've brought a glimpse of Light to this page without overdoing it. but whatever I've done, I'm out of here. Not that I was ever here, of course.

TEN

A TASTE OF BEING BEING

No single arrow I shoot is going to strike home with everyone I use it on, which is why I come to meetings with a full quiver. But if I could only show up with a scant few, what follows would surely be one of them. Let's call it the camera exercise. And what does it do? It gives you a taste of being Being, of standing as awareness.

If you have not yet had an awakening, this is a great way to get an experiential taste of it. One successful experiment is worth more than many thousands of words. If you are in oscillation, this is the fastest way I know to come back to living recognition. In either situation, it's one of the best practices I know.

In this teaching we are pro-practice, but not as a means to some later end. Practices should cause an immediate shift, an immediate clearing. In this teaching, there ain't no later. We use the body and the mind to move beyond both of them. My single criterion is "Does it work?" If so, it goes in the tool box. If it doesn't, throw it into the sea and never mention it again.

First, let's define our terms. When I say "standing" as awareness, what I mean is *consciously* being Being. Right now. We are already the one thing going on, because we can't be anything else. There is nothing else beyond, below, or behind oneness. We all know this. Many of us are sick of hearing about it and dying to experience it. The trick, of course, is that it doesn't feel like we're the one thing going on until it does. Until then, it feels like we're just plain old ordinary us, and for plain old ordinary us, the goal is usually one of connecting to or unifying with oneness.

That would be a reasonable step and a fine goal were it not impossible. We cannot unify with what we already are. We cannot connect to what we already are. In Awakening Sessions, once I have people actively experiencing their true nature —even though they don't yet know it —I will often ask, "Did you have to connect with it?" The answer is inevitably "No." I'll then ask, "Could you actually disconnect from it?" There's a pause, and then, once again, the answer is always a negative. Both unification and connectivity require a minimum of two things, and we are talking about Nonduality, not some sort of elevated dualism.

Being Being is not something we can do later. The only time we can ever be Being is right now, just as the only place to be Being is right here. We cannot wait for the time or space to be "right" in order for us to become what we already are. We simply have to recognize it. Oddly enough, that can be quite a difficult thing to do. Many people spend their entire lives trying to cause a shift that can't ever happen and never needs to. When I say a "shift," what I really mean is the perception of a shift. Think for a moment. How could we ever manage to shift into reality? Does that make any sense? If we look at it closely, it's a ridiculous idea. The better question is, "How could we ever manage to shift out of reality?" The obvious answer is we can't. So we're not trying to make anything new happen, we're just trying to recognize the oldest thing there is: Isness itself!

Suppose that a guy dressed in jeans and a T-shirt, someone I know to be a veteran firefighter, came up and asked me, "How do I become a fireman?" What advice do you think I should offer him? I might start with pointing out the obvious and simply tell him, "Hey, buddy, don't look now, but you're already a fireman." Yet what if that didn't do the trick? Imagine he told me, "Yes, that's what I hear too, but I don't have any sense of being a fireman. I don't feel like a fireman."

In that case, my second approach might be, "Really? You don't? Then why don't you go put on your uniform?" They say "Clothes don't make the man," but clothes certainly give us a wonderful sense of who we are. Is Life so different? Maybe not. From my view it appears that Life has got a whale of a closet! Just on this planet alone, in the outback of a galaxy that's in the outback of the universe, she's got 7,000,000,000 outfits. We call them people. She puts them on and prances around in the mirror admiring herself for a while and has little drama classes with them, but eventually they all wear out. No problem. Old outfits disappear and new ones arise. Poof! Just like that! What a show! And it's all on auto-pilot. No one's doing anything, but everything's being done.

So, let's pretend that you've already heard that "everything is one" (with or without a capital O) for the standard million or so times that we hear that phrase, and it hasn't caused so much as a ripple, much less a breakthrough. Let's go further and suggest that you have read so much about it, talked so much about it, and pursued spiritual practices so much trying to find it, that you've pretty much come to believe this bit of hearsay about oneness. "Okey-dokey, I'm the One. Agreed. Hurray, whoopee. Now what?"

Well, for all you nondual firefighters out there reading this, meaning the majority of you who are taking in these very words in this very moment —yes, even including you

—my advice is that you put on your uniform. You will then be able to get a concrete sense of your firefighterness. You might even see that you always already are a firefighter. Funny hat, big boots, suspenders and all. Hey, look at me! I'm the real deal! Who knew?

Of course you already have your uniform on. You always do. In the absence of your uniform, there may still be a you, but there's no you that you can experience, so forget about casting off your uniform. What I want to do is simply draw your attention to one tiny part of your uniform, and then have you put it on very slowly and deliberately. I want you to wear it consciously instead of unconsciously, which is what you typically do. Here's how.

Do you have a cell phone with a camera in it? Cut the camera on, and then pan it around the room. Do you see how it just records, just registers whatever it sees? What does the camera think about what it's registering? What beliefs does the camera have about what it's recording? How many opinions does the camera hold about what it's registering? What positions is it taking up about what it's recording?

What's that you say? The camera is not thinking at all? It doesn't have any beliefs, opinions, or positions about what it's seeing while panning around? Are you saying that the camera, so to speak, is having a nonconceptual experience of the room? Neat. Why don't you try it?

I want you to use that body —what you erroneously think of as being your exclusive body —as a camera. Your camera. Now pan around the room just as you did with your cell phone, only let that unit be the body of a camera, and let the unit's eyes be the lens. Just like your cell phone's lens, just look. Don't label, don't judge, don't tell any stories about what you're looking at. Just look.

You know that you're alive, do you not? Of course you do. You just simply know that you are. You could say, "I am," and know that you're right, yes? Yes. Now just pretend that you are the one thing going on that you've heard so much about. Look through the body, not as the body. So you have to be looking at yourself now, correct? Do you get that? If not, back up, and read this again until you do get it.

Let's take this slowly. Here's a recap.

1) You are using that body as a camera.
2) You know that you are.
3) You are pretending that you are the one thing going on, and that you are thus looking at yourself.

You know that you are, but when you use that body as a camera, when you look *through* the body, but not *as* the body, do you know what you are? No. Me either. What do you actually know other than that you are? Nothing, right? Same here. I know that I don't know, but that's all I know. How about you?

Can you tell me if there's anything missing, or is what you're looking at always already complete? We could sort of say it's completely complete, could we not? That's the way it is when I do it. How about for you?

51

Now, drop the pretending, and go to your actual experience. For this experiment, suspend your ability to label. When you look without labeling through the body as a camera, how many things are going on in the world that you are filming? When I do it, I count one. If you can't label, you can't judge, can you? In the absence of labeling and thus judging, is there truly any division in whatever it is that you're looking at? Is there any genuine separation? There sure isn't for me, I can tell you that with great confidence.

When you use your body as a camera to view that mysterious scene —because without labels there's not even a "world" —how are things going? How's that whatever-it-is getting along? In the absence of labeling, we can't compare, can we? And in the absence of comparing, can you find a problem? Me either.

When you use that unit as a camera, and YOU are the ONE THING going on, then you are, as they say, NONDUAL, wouldn't you agree? If that's the case, as it certainly is, then what would you say is showing up in your camera? Everything, you say? Yes, that's true. Everything. Is there another word for that, one that really says it with style? How about *What Is*? That's what's showing up, correct? Of course it is. Well, since that's the case, is there anything that really is, that's not showing up? Not for me!

So how about comparisons? Not there, huh? That's because comparisons aren't in What Is. Only real stuff is in What Is. So where do are all comparisons live? In your head. I call that territory *what isn't*. It can't show up in your body-camera because it doesn't exist. It isn't part of What Is, and there's nothing BUT What Is.

How about alternatives? Surely there must be alternatives to What Is? If so, where would they be? Hmmm.. They'd have to be IN What Is, don't you think? If they aren't, where would they be? Ah, in what isn't again! Your head!

How about all those universes and dimensions where woulda-coulda-shoulda mean something? Do they show up? Nope. Then where do they live? In your head. Does the past show up in your lens. Nope. How about the future? Nope. How about that Wonderful Land, the land where what you think about stuff actually matters. Does that show up? Nope. You're stuck with What Is, and in What Is, your beliefs, opinions, and positions mean squat.

How about "someplace else"? Nope. You got your Here, you got your Now, and you got nothing else. That's all that shows up, because that's all that is.

Want to argue with what you see? Okay. How's that working out for you? Are you changing anything, or have you just got what you already had, only now you're suffering over it? Funny how that works, is it not? It only works like that every time. Instead of arguing with What Is, I'd spend my energy looking at how I could get along with It, or open an investigation into how What Is might be in the next moment if I made some practical tweaks.

I think I've made my point. If I haven't, it's unlikely any further illustration will work.

YOU, my friend, are Being. You are always being Being, but this camera exercise will help you to get the sense of being Being, like the firefighter putting on his uniform. Being is where you're always looking from, only sometimes you get confused. You get confused when you look as the body, instead of through it. After all, it's not your exclusive body anymore than any other body is. It's just another unit. It's just another tool for functioning in the dream. It's really quite like my eyeglasses, which are a tool I use for looking through, only my eyeglasses never make the mistake of thinking they're the looker! But when you look through that unit, you make the silly mistake of thinking that you are your looking tool! How funny is that?

Welcome to a taste of being Being. You can do this anytime. You can do this on the fly. It will not transform you, it will dissolve you. Welcome Home.

ELEVEN

WHAT IS AND WHAT ISN'T

You may have heard it many times: There is only what is. Why then do we think there is a what isn't? This imagined sense of *what isn't* co-arises with the imagined sense of an exclusively human identity. This *what isn't* doesn't actually exist, but it feels like it does. Common names for what isn't would be my name, Fred, and your name.

I'm not suggesting that you try not to experience your human identity. I certainly experience Fredness, and since I am Nonduality itself, I am Fredness, but I don't believe I am exclusively Fredness. I am not confused about that.

When I'm not confused about where I'm looking from, I'm not confused about what I'm looking at. When I'm not confused about where I'm looking from, I cannot find anything wrong with What Is, with this current come-and-go arising. I cannot find anything missing. I cannot find anything out of order. I cannot find anything that is appearing either early or late. I cannot find an other. I cannot find alternative universes or dimensions where what I think about What Is actually matters. I'm hung with This, just as it is.

In the absence of imaginary comparisons, i.e., my beliefs, opinions, and positions—in the absence of my being BOPped— I notice that THIS, This that I'm hung with is just fine. I don't even know what it is, but I notice that it's fine. It is as it is. Period. That certainty is missing with what isn't. Common words that arise within what isn't are:

should, could, would; I, you, us, them; then, now; wish, dream, think. Think of some more of your own.

Look closely at your language. Are you describing What Is, or what isn't? You're always describing from where you live. Are you living in What Is, or are you living in what isn't? Are you telling the truth about what's going on, or are you first lying to yourself, pretending that there's a what isn't that you can live in, and then suffering over your own lies?

TWELVE

CLAIMING YOUR TRUE IDENTITY AFTER AWAKENING

I work in Awakening Sessions with people from all over the world, and whether it is an academic from India or a weight lifter from England, once awakening happens, I am likely to offer the same advice. Very seldom is it not appropriate. This advice is one of the most crucial tools I can give to those who wake up in my sessions, whether the awakening has been world shattering or subtle: Claim your true identity. If you don't, you are likely to again become absorbed in the dream.

Truth knows no favorites: absolute equality is the standard. Everyone on the planet has the raw potential for Self-realization at every moment of every day. This is hard to accept, but I promise you that it's true. When we're ready, we "get it". When we're ready, we can't not get it! Some are closer than others. Some are a lot closer than others. A heavy percentage of the people who are drawn to me are simply frustrated and tired out, and that has made them ready. A worn-out ego is more apt to become a compliant ego. It's more likely to take a nap for at least a little while, allowing the children to play at Awakening, but it seldom naps forever.

More often than not, even a tired ego gradually rebuilds and reestablishes itself as the arbiter of reality. Oscillation seems to be the rule in these things; in fact, I can't recall a sure, pure exception. As I have often reported, I was in oscillation for 3 1/2 years and cloudy for 18 months after that. Early on I had no idea that there was anything like a "typical path" that we go through once we've taken that first giant step and find ourselves no longer seekers, but finders. However, that glorious sensation may not last, and when it wanes, we think that "we" have lost "our" enlightenment, though the awakening itself never goes anywhere. We do! This is part of the "typical" path. And yes, there is a typical path.

A key aspect of the typical path is buying the myth that awakening is the end of the road, as I did back in 2006. If you do that, you will be just as disappointed as I was. Here is the embarrassing truth of my own awakening. I believed with all my heart that no one could have ever been here before. I was willing to grudgingly give the benefit of the doubt to perhaps Buddha, and maybe Eckhart Tolle, who was my idol at the time, but probably no one else who had ever existed. This astonishing arrogance is often present in what I will term "brilliant" awakenings. We think we've got it all, and we think it'll last forever. We don't, and it doesn't.

Unity is the truth of things. Diversity, all these lovely arisings, including the one we wrongly think we are, appear within unity. Awakening is typically both an event and a process. After the event of our first sight of truth, we then go, if we are open and willing enough, through the process of moving toward abidance and embodiment. But neither one of those things is likely to be present for quite a while. That's the bad news. The good news is that you won't care! It's not like we ever graduate. We open forever, and so long as we go with the flow of what is, we'll enjoy every step. If we find ourselves thinking we should be more awake than we are, that we should right now be as clear as that time we can almost remember, then we can be assured we are looking at the dream from within the dream, and we will suffer

So let's get back to this prize advice of mine. Why is Claiming Our True Identity the single most critical thing we can do to spur the awakening process? I capitalize that here to make it absolutely clear what it is that I'm talking about. Back in the days when I was a seeker, I could hardly wait for the seeker to wake up—I wanted Fred to wake up so badly. The only problem with that notion is that it's never going to happen. Never. To anyone. Including you, the one reading this right now.

Asking a human unit to wake up is not very different from asking a bowling ball or a paper towel to wake up. These bodies are not nearly so different from those things as we like to think. Now, having said that, let me say that on one hand the human body is a simply marvelous, miraculous object. I'm absolutely crazy about mine, and my wife's too, for that matter. But they're both objects. In the apparent absence of that which inhabits and animates the body, it is of a good deal less value than either a bowling ball or a paper towel! In fact, once the animation leaves the body, we have to bury it or burn it, and pretty quickly, or it'll start to stink and make us sick, too!

It's that which inhabits and animates the body that does the waking up. Call it Life, Tao, God, Brahman, Great Spirit, Holy Spirit, just plain Spirit, Consciousness, Awareness, Awakeness, Being, Tom, Ted, or Sue. Whatever the title, that is the ineffable essence that wakes up: The no-thing which contains and simultaneously is every last arising—from proton, to elephant, to the more obvious living-verbing of a sunset or rainbow— is what wakes up to the dream of the personal self. It wakes up to the dream of selfing. It wakes up to the arising, the event, the pattern that we call Fredness or you-ness.

In that moment of awakening, whether spectacular or subtle, we know ourselves to be the un-One Thing. I say "un-One" because oneness, while being a handy label that I use quite a bit, is not the truth. It merely points toward the truth of un-One, Advaita, not-two. In oscillation, we slip back into thinking we are the little me, the body-mind. We experience a sense of lostness, often of desperation, even dire mental pain because I had something holy and then I lost it. It was here and then it left. How do I get that back? I must get back that great feeling, understanding, peace, or however you label it. I must!

What has happened? One way of saying it is that we are giving up our credentials as finders and picking back up our credentials as seekers. We are right back on the seeking train, only we're riding in a better cabin car. I suggest instead that you claim your True Identity while you are awake. I'll ask people, "You know you're awake, right?" They answer affirmatively. "Do you need to call anyone to verify that for you, or do you know this to be true beyond a doubt?" They know it to be absolutely true and need no outside confirmation, not even mine. The experience is self-confirming. I even lead people through some of the traditional nondual pointers to see how those pointers line up with their current experience. I want there to be no room for doubt later. I don't want them to imagine that I somehow hypnotized them into believing they were awake when they were not.

Once we see the truth of our own experience, why not accept that our True Identity is that of the not-something, not-nothing, No-thing that holds, fills, and is the universe? We want to claim that identity, whether we are cloudy or clear. If we will make the unalterable decision that I am *This*, whatever *This* may be, whatever shape it has currently taken on, both when I can see/be it, and also when I cannot see/be it, I have given myself a huge leg up in the clearing process. Vote for your own experience of What Is, not what your mind says about What Is.

Why do we backslide into the well-worn lie? Only because that's the easiest thing to do, tantalizingly easy. I know. In my case, I had thought myself to be this Fredness for so long and was so familiar with his path that I went back to it with all its suffering because I was not yet ready to live in the unknown. Few if any of us are, not all in one shot. Both clarity and the willingness that clarity spawns come gradually. It took me damn near forever to wake up, but that was only according to the unit's perspective. According to the vastness, it took however long it took—who cares?

We can only bite off what we can bite off at any given time. How much we bite off is essentially insignificant. What matters is that we bite and then hang on like snapping turtles—those creatures that won't let go until it thunders, as the old tales tell us. Let us hang onto our experience, and let our thinking do whatever it wants. Even if we believe ourselves to be the unit, if we ever had any sort of genuine clarity there will be a little piece of us that knows. There will be a part of us that knows that things don't really work as they appear to work. We may even remember that things work exactly 180 degrees away from how we think, but we just can't remember quite how it was that it all looked.

That makes us vulnerable. Ego will likely re-present itself as an "unbiased observer" of the Way Things Are, which is code for how things could, should or would be if we lived in a world where what we think about What Is actually counts. Clearly we do not. If you are in an argument with What Is, you are in the dream. If you are in an argument what What Is, you are insane. Come back, come back, come back to the sanity of knowing that there is only What Is, and that outside of imagination, there never were, are, or are going to be any alternatives to What Is. We go with it suffering and leaving claw marks behind us, or we go with it peacefully, perhaps even joyfully, but we are going to go with it regardless. In the end, What Is rules. But only always.

So, if you have a so-called awakening experience and discover who you really are, my invitation to you is to accept what you've found as exactly what it is: the truth. In this way you can dump seeking, or reseeking as I like to call it, right here and now and begin the new journey toward greater and greater clarity. With that attitude, you are working from Awakeness, as Awakeness, without resistance. More clarity will show up much sooner. I'm not saying this is always easy, but I can say that it always works. Clouds or no clouds, the sun is always shining, my friends. It never goes anywhere, we can't actually lose it, and it's always, always shining. You are that sun, the very light of the world.

Claim your identity.

THIRTEEN

AN EXAMPLE OF CLAIMING YOUR TRUE IDENTITY AFTER AWAKENING

After reading "Claiming Your True Identity After Awakening," one of my clients wrote me to say, "You didn't tell us how to do it!"

"There is no 'how,'" I replied. "You just do it."

As unhelpful as my answer sounds, it really is the truth. Asking how to claim your identity is like asking how to surrender. There is no "how" to that either. When you reach either enough pain or enough clarity, you just do it.

When you wake up, at the moment you are really clear—when you know the truth of your being beyond the shadow of a doubt—claim that as your true identity from then on, regardless of whether you're cloudy or clear. As I often say, the sun is always shining. Claim that sun as yourself. Claim that shining as yourself.

Oscillation is simply part of the awakening process. It's not the wrong part; there is no wrong part. It's just another experience for Being to experience. Don't resist it, don't fight it, don't try to hang onto awakeness. Just let it do what it's going to do. It's going to do that anyway! If you're not in line with that you'll suffer, not just over the sense of disconnection but over the sense that it "shouldn't be."

Seeking, initial and subsequent awakenings, oscillation, early stability, abidance, and embodiment are all part of the process. Everybody is different. With every opening, you get as much as you can stand at that moment. This thing is much, much larger than we can imagine. There's no way the mind can stretch to encompass it.

Simply cooperate with the inevitable. That's the fastest way to get clear, and it's the least painful to boot.

Along those lines I want to share an email relating to the topic of claiming. I have the writer's permission to share it and am reprinting it here unedited, except for a couple of typos I corrected. This is an email from Mike, who lives in Australia and got up at 6 a.m. on Friday morning, his time, for our session at what was 4 p.m. Thursday EDT, my time. You have to love that kind of devotion to the truth. It pays off, too.

Mike had what I term a "brilliant" awakening. I see a fair number of them, but it's certainly the exception and not the rule. What I mean by a "brilliant awakening" is that not only is there immediate clear seeing but deep seeing as well, which is reasonably or very well sustained over a period of time. Mike was an interesting case because he had experienced a glimpse of his true being earlier in his life, but he had not claimed his identity.

Subject: Hi from Mike in Oz

Hi Fred,

First, thank you so much for giving of your time on Friday (my time!!) for our conversation together. At all times I felt in safe and loving hands. I cannot recall at what time you sensed that I had "got it" and I never had that "Oh my God" overwhelming feeling, but your floating me off the chair and taking things away until there was nothing more to take away, leaving just the body-less "me" and Being, the "I am", was the lightbulb moment for me with the quiet realisation that "I am Being" and that all things thereafter were arising in me. To that point, while I had read that, it hadn't resonated, wasn't "owned". With each "giving back" in your story, I saw with increasing clarity that every 'thing" is an arising in that which I am. The final piece of the jig saw – at least, the final piece in this section of the jigsaw fell into place.

For that, more thanks than I can adequately express.

Thereafter, if you picked up any change in me, then it wasn't wholly due to anything you said – it was in large part due to the fact that I realised that I was bloody cold!! The temperature outside the house was minus two, and I had forgotten to turn on the heater before we started! The room was freezing – after we signed off, it took two coffees and a bit of early sunlight warmth before full functioning started to return!!

I read somewhere where realization, while it may come "out of the blue" needs a context within which to be appreciated fully. In some, that context may be supplied by a guru, teacher or friend. Without these, what happens can go unnoticed "like a thief in the night" and not be, at the time appreciated for what it is. For this unit, the whatever-it-was that left me knowing that "everything is going to be OK" [Mike is referring here to his previous glimpse] might well have been a realisation – but I didn't have any context to possibly explain what that might have been – and so it went unexplained and (outwardly at least) unappreciated.

Thereafter, reading, watching videos, listening to interviews started to provide a context – but such is the lot of dualistic activity that I couldn't be sure that any emerging context (or philosophy, or story) was good, bad or indifferent. It was only in the last month or so that I started to realise that contexts are ALL misleading and that only that which remains after all contexts/stories etc. are seen through as irrelevant and misleading is the truth. Life, This – right here and right now. It was at this point, needing clarity, that I discovered (was led to) your site, and the rest – as they say – is history.

There is no expectation of residing in Oneness 24/7. In my previous stumbling about I have thought that I have got it/lost it innumerable times and so am prepared for that oscillation to continue until it doesn't. I now have a rock-solid knowing of Being – my true state – and know that, while it might be temporarily obscured, it is always here. I just need to let go and relax back into it. Rest assured that if cloudiness ever starts to alarm me, I will book in with you for a "tune up"!

Thank you again.

As One,

Mike

FOURTEEN

HOW DO THINGS LOOK WHEN WE'RE SEEING FROM TRUTH?

Here is more seeing from Mike in Australia. He sent me this email shortly after his Awakening Session with me. What's great is that Mike is one of those rare people who can adroitly speak about his experience, and is also a good writer.

Here's his unedited letter.

From Mike in Oz

Hi Fred,

Just over a month ago you took me through [an Awakening Session], at the conclusion of which you invited me to keep in touch. It's been long enough for me to gather a few coherent impressions (and a question) together – so here goes!!

For starters, any sense that "I am this unit" has gone. If I look for "where has the "me" gone", there is no sense of it being anywhere. In fact, the futility of even trying to locate "me" is very obvious. So I've given up even thinking about "the sense of me might return" How can something that doesn't exist make a return appearance? The concept of "me" is irrelevant. There is no need to "kill it off" or even stun it into submission. If it appears, it appears. If it doesn't, it doesn't. Simple.

Which is not to say that the me-that-doesn't-exist hasn't made a surprise appearance at times. It occasionally shows, but so too does the certain knowledge that I'm not that which has made the surprise appearance. It's almost as if I'm beyond the me and can see the me doing its thing with an attitude of tolerance and affection. It's not a sense of being a separate observer, but rather of an observing. Sort of "there's silly Mike doing something dumb." Only once did cloudiness linger – when Mike got cranky over something – and the knowledge that "I'm not that" took a few minutes to kick in. When it did, the me faded, and peace returned.

The seeker died with the [our session] and has not returned. That is a mixed blessing in some ways, as I quite enjoyed surfing the internet, or reading books to find the answer to some spiritual-type question. There is simply no urge to find the answers to anything – which sounds boring but is very gratifying. I still visit some "spiritual" sites, but not with a fevered focus. I sort of "graze" through them without feeling that I have to act on what is written or viewed.

The acceptance of what is simply happening is deepening. I no longer look for the "answer" or a "sign" either "out there" or "in here" I just take what appears. Sometimes that means that I'm aware of stuff that's "good" and sometimes I'm aware of stuff that's "not so good." There's no sense that the good stuff must be encouraged or the bad stuff pushed away – what is, is what is!

I guess one of the stereotypical expectations of a "seeker" is that things will be different after the realisation of what I am dawns. My experience is that things still look the same, but that the relationship to whatever appears is subtly different. I guess I could say that there is awareness that nothing that appears is of a long-lasting or separate nature to that which is seeing. But trees, birds, people, buildings and cars still appear exactly as they did before awareness dawned – and that's a relief if only because it adds to the ordinary pleasure of everyday life. I have read some pretty nihilistic impressions of "what is after realisation" looks like. I'm relieved that life continues as life always has (because, I guess, that which is has no time dimension and has always been unchanging, perfect in it's very being).

My relationship with other people has changed insofar as there is no desire to change whatever they're doing, but rather a loving tolerance that whatever they're doing is what they're meant to be doing. There is no reason why they should be doing anything else. Previously, when someone did something stupid, I would quietly rail about their stupidity and what they should be doing. Now I simply observe without feeling the need to do anything about it. Life is sweet.

I have a question. In *The Book of Undoing*, you have a scene where you take Brooke through the seeing that a lamp is not separate from her, but that "she" is joined to "the lamp. I read that just before our [session] and I guess a pre-[session] expectation of post-[session] clarity is that I should see myself in objects external to this unit. I didn't and that bugged me for a while. I know that all is Oneness, that I am that and that apparently separate objects have no long-lasting or independent nature. Every apparent 'thing' is an expression as Oneness.

64

But the gate of vision is powerful and I got hung up on the word "seeing." I know the lamp is not, in truth, a separate object from that which I am – but the eyes still portray a separate lamp that I am seeing. Did Brook visually meld into the lamp (as a seen expression of oneness) or did Brook know that the lamp, in truth has no existence separate from consciousness/Being/Oneness and therefore came to realise that "distance from something" is a concept which in truth has no meaning – there is no separate place, just as there is no dimension of time. There is just here, right now. I'd appreciate your clarifying this for me. Am I missing something? If I am, I need a clarity session with you!!

That's probably enough for one email – I could rattle on, but I will stop

In continuing gratitude and love,

Mike

I am grateful for Mike's beautifully clear letter. His question points to a troublesome issue experienced by many who have had awakenings, even profound ones like Mike's. This is very subtle stuff, so I'm going to pick it apart. It may seem that I am being needlessly hard on Mike, who has awakened so beautifully, but these issues are among the stickiest. They don't go down easily.

Let's be clear, Mike felt he should see himself in objects, but he didn't, so he felt something was missing. Let's examine this on a couple of levels.

First off, Mike says "I should see myself in objects." Who's talking here? Does Awareness really feel "should" about anything? Or is Mike-who-doesn't-really-exist calling from the sidelines? See how subtle identification can be? Our stories are extraordinarily sticky, and few of us—none that I know—wake up into sparkling clarity. Whenever a "should" comes into your mind after awakening, consider the source.

A second belief hiding in Mike's question is that his experience should be like Brook's. Is that true? Says who? Awareness, or Mike-who-doesn't-really-exist? Where's the benchmark for that assumption? In Mike's head, maybe?

Let's look at yet a third belief hiding behind that idea that Brook saw or felt something Mike didn't. It suggests the belief that all experiences of awakening are the same or should be the same. Is that true? Where's the benchmark for that assumption? Is it not just an opinion that's arising within Awareness, which Mike-who-doesn't-really-exist is grabbing hold of and claiming?

It is my experience that every awakening is like a snowflake, absolutely unique. This is because every unit that awakening comes through is absolutely unique, and the unit's conditioning, both hard (DNA) and soft (the accumulation of post-birth conditioning) colors the awakening experience. The most awake being on the planet is still one step removed from truth. It may be a tiny step for some, but so long as there's a body, there's a step. There may be the subtle underlying gnawing sense that, "There is something missing from 'my' Oneness." Is that true? Who feels that?

Let's look specifically at what Mike feels is missing from his awakening: Mike feels he should see himself in objects, but he doesn't. Is that "should" true? Let's review what Brook went through.

First, Brook looks at the lamp and discovers no actual line of separation between what's looking and what's being looked at. Brook finds only a single continuum, which exists without division of any kind.

Second, Brook, who is by this time already awake and knows there is no separation, is asked if there is still a sense of distance between her and the lamp and answers, "Yes." Brook is then asked what causes the sense of distance between the seer and the lamp and answers, "The space."

So Brook feels a "sense" of distance. Let's look at what a sense of something really is. My favorite example is that I could be in a dark room and be just fine until I suddenly get a sense that there's a snake in the room. I believe that thought. My body starts to sweat and hyperventilate from fear. And then someone pops on a light, I see there's no snake in the room, and I let out a huge sigh of relief as my body begins to calm down. I say, "What a relief! I had a sense there was a snake in the room, but there's no reality to back that up! All is well!"

Brook reports that regardless of enlightenment, there is still a sense of distance between Brook and the lamp, due to the space. Just as I believed my thought that there was a snake in the room, Brook is believing a thought, which is "Space is separating everything from everything else." But is it true?

I ask Brook to look at the lamp again and to notice that space is not what's dividing everything from everything else; rather, it's what is connecting everything to everything else. And at that point, something shifts for Brook and that shift shows Brook, with a little nudging from me, that there is no real line separating Brook and the lamp. And I ask, "If there's no line between the two, then are there really two?" And Brook acknowledges that there cannot be two.

At that point in a session of this sort a client may—or may not—experience a visual shift. Some do, some don't. I experience one every time I take the trouble to do this exercise. I never experience one by just thinking about it. But, it doesn't matter whether we do or don't. We get a clear message anyway: there is only one without a second.

But remember that Mike's disappointment came because he was not seeing himself in other objects the way Brook did, but Brook never said that. Brook said there was no line of division, so in this case, Mike's phrasing of the issue added to the confusion. It creates the image of some individual seeing him or herself physically reflected in an external object; however, if there only one without a second, what is there to see and who is there to see it? The seer is the seen.

Some spiritual experiences involve all diversity being erased, but those states are not practical for everyday living, and they are no more valid than your experience of peeling a potato. Of course, we don't go around melded into things all the time. Our experience is like the well known optical illusion of the faces and the cup. Cup or face, face or cup? What you get is what you see, but the source is the same. Just accept what is seen with the knowledge that you are both the aware space that all things appear to and the appearances that arise in that space: one without a second.

FIFTEEN

A DAY IN THE LIFE OF AWAKENESS

Occasionally I'm asked how my post-awakening perceptions differ from my pre-awakening perceptions. To be perfectly candid, I can't remember a lot of what it used to be like. I know there was a lot of confusion and suffering. Today there is no pull toward actively referencing that or even remembering it. That was then and This is Now.

Of course, as I work with my clients I see a reflection of myself as I was, so the memories are certainly still there, and sometimes comparison happens, but it's completely passive, never active. Those memories are like bubbles that are dislodged by some arising in my experience. When that happens, they float to the top and are noticed, but in my day-to-day life I don't consciously compare this current experience to any other time or place. I see that comparison sometimes happens, but it's generally brief and is not taken seriously.

For me, there isn't anything other than my current experience—no other time, no other place, no alternatives to What Is, and no exceptions to that rule. The living truth of right here, right now is what is seen and experienced. Reality is simple. The dream is both involved and involving, but prior to measurement or argument there is just This. Upon this simple background of unity we invent a center (the personal me) and then project a world (our own), which houses genuine diversity, but only apparent division. Buying into the separation thing is actually optional. Our suffering is always trying to tell us that. As bizarre as it seems, suffering is our friend. It's our cue that we're not awake.

The first large psychological move that a baby human makes is the acceptance of the story of division. We're told that there's a me over here and a world over there. The moment we accept that agreement, and we all do, we set ourselves up to ride the roller coaster of our newly forming dream. Next comes classification and valuation, which we commonly refer to as judgment, which is the tool we use to evaluate the world we just invented.

I no longer spend much time in the dream. I chiefly live *in* This and *as* This with occasional forays into the dream of self and suffering. I'm still perfectly capable of identifying with my character and falling back into the dream; I just don't stay there very long when I do. So far. I don't want to get cocky.

What about tomorrow? Who knows? I am not a subscriber to the idea of permanent enlightenment. Who would have that? A me? What I see is the opportunity for ongoing enlightenment, to be awake to this moment, and this arising, and then the next, and the next, and the next.

Meanwhile, this unit does what it does, and I stand helplessly by while it does it. I can see that the unit is a whole lot more skillful than it used to be. I always welcome progress, and I never scold What Is for being as it is. Positive reinforcement is the only way to promote positive change without raising new judgments and resistance to get hung up in. I catch myself doing stuff right and then I celebrate it. But enough generalities; let me get to specifics.

When I wake up in the morning, it feels very much as it always did, except that I'm neither hung over, nor in trouble, and my mind is not relentlessly playing the single reel movie of the Awful Story of Fred. There is no sense of either Fred or dread.

Instead, I open my eyes to find a little white dog and a small tabby cat curled up on either side. They are lovely, free beings. I saw long ago that I was their caretaker, not their owner. They have taught me a lot about love and poop. There's no such thing as a one-ended stick: it's all or nothing.

We have another cat as well, and all three animals each have their personal issues—as do Betsy and I. But none of us requires one of the others to change in order to be accepted or valued. If change happens in, or to, one of us, we all immediately incorporate it. If it doesn't, that's fine too.

You get to be yourself here. It's not a plan or an open agreement, it's just what happens. It always has been, even in pre-awakening. But don't think awakening won't change your relationship with animals. They feel it faster than we do—and they like it! A lot.

It's quite difficult for me to get out of bed in the morning, and it's not just because of the friendly animals or my typical late-night hours. Most mornings I wake up with waves of energy rolling up through my feet and legs, sometimes through my whole body. I won't lie: it is entirely delicious. Energy has been a big factor in my spiritual story since well prior to my first large awakening in 2006. Some mornings I just can't come up with a good reason as to why I should ever again move, so I lie there completely powerless until the body finally gets up of its own accord

I stumble downstairs to the kitchen, whereupon it is immediately obvious that I'm in a stage set. This is true 100% of the time, of course, but I usually notice it most profoundly in my kitchen in the morning or if I'm down there alone late at night. In the morning, the light is special in the kitchen, and late at night I am especially wide open, but whatever the reasons, Shakespeare was spot on about stages and plays and a great deal more.

All the world's a stage,

And all the men and women merely players;

They have their exits and their entrances,

And one man in his time plays many parts...

Anyway, back in the kitchen, I move on about fixing a cup of coffee—except when I don't. Sometimes an object, or a portion of the set will catch my attention, and I am frozen. In that moment of sudden brightness, I have no clue what it is that I'm looking at, but I am riveted, stunned, nailed to the floor. Call it awe. And then the body fixes coffee. It's easy to get lost in a mug of coffee, too, what with the steam rising from the black pool of endless depth and mystery.

On a good morning, meaning a morning when my schedule isn't screaming for me, I sit in my big chair in the living room, drink coffee, and either pet whichever animal hops up or simply stare softly out the window. It is heaven. I then read from Emerson, Nisargadatta, or a scripture of some sort, or better yet, all three when I have the time. Often I will close my eyes and sit quietly for a few minutes. I don't do it in the hope of making something happen; I do it to help me deeply notice what's already happening.

On many mornings I'll have either an Awakening Session or a Clarity Session beginning at either 10:00 or 11:00. I never go into these sessions with the idea that I am going to teach; rather, I simply open myself to sitting before the computer monitor to watch and learn. I pull up my background Skype screen, cut on my stage lights, dial somebody up, and then talking happens—or at least it has so far.

But I didn't earn this gift, and I certainly don't control it. I don't use it; it uses me. What comes out of my mouth is as fresh to my ear as it is to the client's. While there is a general direction to every session, each one is unique. They tailor themselves to meet the client precisely where he or she is. I have no idea how any of it works. With my track record being what it is, if it's a Awakening Session, I foolishly expect the miracle—for my client to awaken—and they almost always do.

How? I don't know. Interestingly the unit thinks this is all cut and dry—it's completely underwhelmed by this show of apparent magic. It just wants me to hurry so that it doesn't miss lunch!

If it's a weekend, I may have someone coming to my house for a meeting. I like these most. Often a current client, or student, or friend, depending upon how they refer to themselves, will accompany a friend to make the introduction, and to piggy-back on the Awakening Session. The new person hears everything for the first time while the established client sits quietly and hears everything for the next time. That's a good thing.

Repetition is the mother of clarity.

I welcome my guests, perhaps we get something to drink, sit down, and then I have them tell me the five-minute version of their spiritual story to give me an idea of where I'm starting from. We then launch right in. Two hours later the freshly awakened client, the established client, and I all go to lunch. The unit is still not impressed, because it knows it's not the one doing it. It is rather jealous, I think.

Sounds just like a unit, does it not?

Lunch lasts an hour or more, and it's always enjoyable. I hold forth, talking about the ramifications of awakening, or I answer questions, tell stories or something, and then the clients go home. I head upstairs to my study where I go to work on teaching chores, such as answering email, writing for or making adjustments and improvements to my website, *Awakening Clarity Now*, or perhaps working on a book-in-progress.

I have to tell you, it's all quite weird to have this thing thrust on you. It's not a bad gig, but it drives me from morning to midnight. The energy I had as a seeker was transferred to my search for greater clarity in post-awakening, and has now found a home in taking this teaching out into the world.

I usually shower in the afternoons, and when I do, it's always a dice roll because I never know how long it's going to take. Sometimes I step in, become totally lost in the sensations of heat and water and closeness, and stay until the water begins to cool. I frequently get out having no clue if I have fully bathed or not, but it's always a beautiful experience. Yet when I dry my hair I sometimes discover that I haven't shampooed it.

Betsy usually comes home from work about 6:30 during the week, earlier on weekends. If it's a weekday, I will typically not have seen anyone in the flesh all day. We have dinner together and talk excitedly. We never tire of each others' company, we never argue, and we are almost always like a pair of enthusiastic chipmunks who've just run into a large field of ripe nuts.

We take nothing for granted, especially not each other. We light candles every night, and play music such as solo piano or guitar in the background. We say grace at every in-house meal, because it's a lovely human thing to do. It's a way of expressing gratitude, and it's a ritual that brings us closer together. And we always slip the animals some of our food.

After dinner we read or watch an hour-long DVD of something very English while lying in bed holding hands. We are both hopeless anglophiles. She's asleep by 8:30 or 9:00 in the evening, and I'm back to being on my own. I often do a second shift of writing. Ours is a small quiet life, but it is a deep one.

Most days, other than during session work, I'm by myself 21 hours, which is lovely. Don't get me wrong—I'm crazy about my wife, but I also love being alone. So does she. That's a good thing, because we don't get to spend all that much time with each other. She is a selfless worker bee, and I, in effect, am a married hermit with a webcam.

I get lost a lot during the day. The extraordinary ordinary is endlessly fascinating. Anything can capture my attention. For example, whenever I look at a ceiling, any ceiling, I am instantly enchanted. It's a world I don't usually pay much attention to, but when I do, it briefly grabs my full attention

There is a huge Yellow Jessamine vine on my porch. Sometimes I step outside and am completely taken by the winding stems and arching leaves. Fantastic. I feed the birds up front and out back, and they are forever stealing my focus. I know some of their proper names, but I'm not much of a birder, merely a lover of birds. I just gawk at the ones I don't recognize, wondering how anything can be so perfect.

I used to drive a lot. I traveled three states looking for good books to buy, but things have changed since I woke up. It's pretty obvious that the universe would rather I serve as a spiritual teacher instead of a bookseller, so I've closed out the book business. I'm happy to serve in any capacity I'm pulled toward. About that driving. When I go to the post office, or the dentist, or the grocery store, I am always captivated by how I am driving through myself. The car and the unit move, spaciousness stays reliably still, and I am the whole kit and kaboodle. I actually don't need a car at all unless I want to pretend that I'm in motion. As it so happens, I like to pretend that nearly every day, so I'd better hang onto the car.

I forget to eat a lot of meals, and I get too busy to sleep as much as the body needs. So the unit finally went on strike after years of general overwork, and two years of burning the candle at both ends to get this teaching established. It wasn't my idea, but it's my responsibility.

I lost a lot of weight, looked haggard, began to get confused and forgetful, and could sense that I was dwindling in a serious way. I went to the doctor and had a full battery of tests; I suspected cancer, just as I always do when I'm losing weight. The unit knows it's a miracle that it's lived this long, and it's always waiting for the other shoe to drop. Luck has been with me so far, and this time I came out clean

I would like to live a long time, but only if I do. I don't want Betsy to be alone. I want the animals to be taken good care of. But from my own perspective, when the unit wants to check out, I'm fine with it. I'm still fond of this unit, and still very interested in it, and it's quite a funny little duck on the oddest of trails, but I'm not particularly attached to it.

Once it's fully seen that the unit is not us, and that we are not it, one's wishes and dreams are seen to be rather hollow, though still a whole lot of fun. Better to focus on right now, whether it's living fully or dying consciously. When I drop my opinions, which I do most of the time, I notice that everything is always going along splendidly, however Life is displaying itself.

Now let me share some of what I've learned from my own experience and the many people I've worked with. This is a little dicey, because when we begin the spiritual path, we really have no idea where it's going to lead us. Some of it will probably be beautiful. Some of it will surely be ugly. And whether we end up cherished, as the Buddha was, tormented like Jesus, or somewhere in the middle, is anyone's guess.

What I can tell you is that both of those extremes are rare. There may be unpleasant stages, but in the end I can report that I'm tickled to death to have had the great blessing of coming to consciously know myself. So far as I know, I don't have any unhappy clients who've woken up—which doesn't mean I couldn't.

Spiritual awakening is the single most important thing that can ever happen to, or more accurately, happen through a human being. It is the apex of human experience. A radical transformation takes place in an instant, and that transformation continues so long as we are open and willing. Awakening is both event and process.

It is sometimes said that there's nothing in it for the ego when we awaken. That statement may indeed be true, but ego is just a part of human complexity. There's a great deal in it for the greater part of the human assembly, which is utilized so that Being can have the incredible experience of watching itself unfold in and as the manifested world. Metamorphosis is the whole point, so to speak.

Absolutely anything can happen in the dream at absolutely any time, and there are no guarantees. Yet there can be, and typically are, both broad and deep practical benefits for the people who come to Self-realization, especially those who successfully orient and become reasonably stable within the new apparent state. Opening to truth is forever—we never graduate—and everyone's realization is different, but here are some of the more common positive changes people report.

Not everyone is going to experience all of these side effects, but everyone will experience at least some of them.

We begin to:

1. Drop our endless spiritual seeking.

2. Discover who we really are.

3. Live free.

4. Find out our real identity.

5. Inherit peace of mind and heart.

6. Uncover a calm center that we never knew existed.

7. Begin to see things as they really are.

8. Learn to embrace life as it really is, right here, right now.

9. Experience greatly diminished psychological suffering.

10. Lower daily stresses significantly.

11. Become willing to live life fully.

12. Drop the fears of failure and success.

13. Lose our anxiety over death.

14. Overcome many common fears.

15. Open to the secret of Oneness.

16. Lower or eliminate our innate sense of lack.

17. Unleash an unexplainable inner joy.

18. See incredible beauty in common objects and ordinary events.

19. Enjoy improved relationships.

20. Learn to control the one thing we can control.

21. Cease to resist life's current.

22. Notice our life patterns.

23. Solve life's deepest mysteries.

24. Get rid of old anger and resentments.

25. Learn to more easily forgive and accept ourselves and others.

26. Live in gratitude.

27. See through the disabling trinity of guilt, shame, and blame.

28. Dump our victim persona.

29. Stop rehearsing the future.

30. Stop reliving the past.

I hope this look into my life as Awakeness has been helpful. If not, don't fret: something else is already arising. After all, everything comes and goes.

Except, of course, *You.*

SIXTEEN

CLARITY IS A TWO-WAY STREET

Spiritual teachings may be telling us the truth, the whole truth, and nothing but the truth, but we're only going to get what we get until we're ready to receive more. This is what Jesus meant when he said, "He who hath ears, let him hear." It's not all up to our teachers. Most of it is not up to them. Most of it is up to us.

For example, sacred literature can only reveal to us what we're already prepared to see, whether it was written a thousand years ago or the day before yesterday. There is a wealth of terrific information and a ton of fabulous pointers in plain sight every day. We can't see them until we can. We don't understand them until we do. Yet once awakening occurs, things that were previously stupefyingly vague and arcane become as clear and solid as glass. Of course, all that arcane stuff is then replaced with new esoterica we don't understand, but that's both the nature and the joy of the game.

The same goes for our teachers and mentors. They don't make clear sense until they do. Our relationship with teachers is rather like the Mark Twain story about a boy and his father: the older the son got, the smarter his father seemed to get! The longer we pursue the spiritual quest with a teacher, the smarter he or she will seem to get—all because we grew a new set of ears. So, whether we get our information and pointers from life itself, or from books, practices, or teachers, the same rule applies. In the interests of brevity, I'll stick with teachers.

In the United States, we are a people in a hurry. We are like a nation of cats: we want to be wherever we aren't. We want to start a practice or work with a teacher just so we can graduate. I think this is a problem not just in the U.S. but in the world at large, and it is such a no-win approach. If we're not established in Nondual awareness and our teacher is, we shouldn't minimize the theoretical gulf between us. Patience and earnestness are critical if we want to walk through the Gateless Gate and join our teacher. The good news is that this apparent wide gulf simply means the teacher has a lot to offer us. As one of my mentors says, we don't want to be in the position of following someone who's twenty minutes ahead of us. You may get some helpful directions, but the perspective will be limited.

Now that I've made that flat statement, let me swoop in and take it away as well. Many of us begin as followers of the really well-known teachers. I'll wager that Eckhart Tolle has reached more people on the planet than just about all the rest of them put together. And if you're Jim Carey or Oprah Winfrey, I'm sure Eckhart is a very cool person to hang out with. But how about us? Most of us are neither rich nor famous, so we won't come near to even meeting Eckhart, much less getting any direct teaching from him. I'm using Eckhart as the example here, simply because he's so well known, but a similar situation exists with Adyashanti, Gangaji, Byron Katie, and a few other big names. I love these teachers, and they are great for getting you started, but the average person can't go one-on-one with them, and that is a crucial problem.

The difference between walking this path with a one-on-one teacher or with a big name you'll never chat privately with for an hour or two or ten is beyond large: it's unfathomable. I never had a one-on-one teacher until after I woke up, and the cloudy awakeness of those early years cannot compare to the clarity and stability that teachers have helped me find. If we have a teacher, our journey is also less likely to remain being about ego. Nearly all of us start with egoic spiritual desires. That's fine, it's a stage. What matters is where we end up. Teachers can help us stay out of that stew by calling us on unconscious thinking or behavior.

It's nice to get outside confirmation of what we're experiencing and where we are along the path. It's important to realize that without a teacher we're trying to guide ourselves to a place we've never been. No wonder it's so difficult! Is confirmation necessary? No. Is it generally beneficial? Oh yes. For one thing, it gives us confidence that, as I shared with a friend recently, "We aren't just sitting in our living room smoking hash."

Ego is more than happy to grant confirmation of all our grandiose notions of where we are on the path and what's going to happen when we're discovered. Such a seeker is more likely to be found out than to be discovered. From the beginning of our journey, ego has been looking forward to being enlightened and is happy as all get out when it decides it's gotten there! Oh, the specialness of it! This is always a false reading; no exception granted.

There's no problem in being either a seed or a sapling. All great trees were once the same. Trouble only starts if a seed or a sapling begins to believe it's already a tree. We can do a lot of damage to ourselves and others if we end up in that position. And it's all too easy to stay there, because the only way we can get out of it is to admit we're wrong. Who wants to do that? The willingness to jettison "rightness" and "righteousness" is not common, and neither is the humility required to remain in an open, not-knowing space of being.

There are no laws in any of this. Awakeness can and does work anyway it wants to, any time it wants to. Having said that, it's fair to say that the very good general directions handed out by well-known spiritual teachers may not work well for us and if they do work, they almost certainly will not work for us indefinitely. The further we go, the more specific information we're going to need. Once we awaken, we're still going to be able to benefit tremendously from guidance, and media may not be the best place to get it—unless, of course, it's the only place we can get it. We may need a sharper finger, one that knows something about where we are on the path and in our lives, to do some pointing for us.

There are plenty of good teachers available if we're simply willing to do our part and avail ourselves of them. Sadly, ego often prefers the famous face on You Tube because then there's no close scrutiny of our thinking and seeing, and we get to magically advance to any level we wish, just as fast as we want! Sadly, we also get to pay the ultimate price for that, which is suffering.

It's certainly not the famous teachers' fault that they may ultimately become limited in their value to us. No matter how awake they may be, no matter their long experience, they are still human beings. Human beings come with limitations, and time is one of them. How can you be on a personal level with thousands, tens of thousands, or even hundreds of thousands of followers? It's impossible. We can influence that many people, and we can sort of obliquely steer a crowd that size, but on most paths a much more personal touch is needed if we're really going to get where we're going. Unless it isn't. I don't say lightning never strikes through a famous teacher, but why bet on that slim possibility?

If we're genuinely sincere, if we really want to wake up and then go beyond that initial opening, then we probably want to place ourselves firmly in the hands of the Law of Large Numbers: we want to do what the majority of people are doing who are getting concrete results.

Lesser known teachers are available worldwide. They are awake, talented, devoted, and for the most part good at what they do. Don't assume lesser-known teachers are less awake than their better-known counterparts. Some of them may even be sharper. You won't know until you sit with them. Given some time, any currently awake teacher can help the great majority of as-yet-unawakened seekers; there's no question about that. And remember, progress in Nonduality is measurable. We're awake, or we're not. Others are waking up around us with the guidance of our teacher, or they're not. Clarity is a better measure than charisma.

As we tread the paths most seekers try out, we want to use our common sense to guide us. We don't ever "give ourselves up or over" to a teacher or a teaching. My advice is not to follow any teacher or teaching suggesting such a thing. Awakeness would never ask for that sort of concession, though a teacher's ego might relish the idea. We are lost before we begin if we give up our good sense. If we surrender, we surrender to what the teacher represents, not the human being who happens to be delivering it. We want to use a teaching to help us cross the ocean, not fall in love with an anchor. We can love and respect our teachers and their teachings without getting stupid. After all, it's our path; let's take some responsibility for it.

Clarity is a two-way street.

SEVENTEEN

TWO REASONS YOU'RE NOT AWAKE ANYMORE

"How come I keep going back into believing that I am the body?" I get this question a lot. A seeker gets a clear vision of his or her beautiful clear essence and then for some reason is suddenly back to believing he or she is that clunky body again. The issue is misidentification. Why does it happen? Why can't we keep our eye on the prize?

One issue that deserves a close look is *Time In Story versus Time in Truth*. In my case, the story of Fredness has been here for sixty-plus years. The knowledge of Truth has been here, in conventional time, for less than eight. The idea that Fredness should automatically "fall away" after a glimpse of Truth or even after a day or a year of seeing Truth is nothing short of absurd. It's clear to me that vestiges of Fredness will be here until this body dies. There may not be any Fred at the heart of the story, but Fredness is still dancing its way along, which is fine. It simply is what it is. See how quick and painless surrender can be?

While I confess to being nothing short of appalled by Fredness's lack of skillfulness from time to time, when I really examine that response I discover that it's Fredness that is appalled by Fredness! Awakeness is never appalled by Fredness. It welcomes Fredness exactly as it is, just like it does everything else. This Fredness unit is not special in a positive or negative way. It's one more potato in the bag.

It's only Fredness's fantasies about how an "enlightened Fred"—as if there could be such thing!—either behaves or should behave that causes upset. But where's the basis in truth for that fantasy? It's nothing more than an opinion over which Fredness will continue to suffer until he doesn't.

Awakeness, unlike Fredness, is totally accepting. Always. We could go so far as to say that acceptance is what Awakeness is! That description is not quite true, as no description of Awakeness is, but it's closer to the truth and is a good deal less grandiose than most descriptions. It's best to keep our descriptions of Awakeness as simple and direct as possible, because nobody likes to polish up the definition of our True Nature more than ego. Why? The more it can polish, the more glare it can create, which helps ego stay separate. Ego loves to confound simple seeing.

In all likelihood, you have had an ego for a lot longer than you have had a sense of your True Nature. Unless you are the rare exception, that ego will be making trouble for some time. Even after an awakening experience, ego keeps offering a lot of seemingly delicious options. The only option it doesn't truly offer is the option to turn itself off. That must come with surrender because only ego thinks it can control what's happening.

There is, however, some good news. Everyone on the planet is at every moment operating from their highest spiritual understanding. That includes the bad guys, even the maniacs. Fortunately, it also includes us, so at least on one level we're off the hook, and seeing clearly that we are where we need to be is part of the answer to the problem of misidentification. Try consciously accepting your current state, ego and all, and see what happens. If your intentions are proper, you may find yourself falling into unconscious identification less and less often.

Speaking of intentions, let me say that in spite of a lot of buzz to the contrary, intentions are critical to your awakening process. They are a second factor in why seekers fall back into misidentification. If you oscillate, take a look at your *Integrity of Intent*.

How much of your precious time and attention are you spending on raising the level of your spiritual understanding? We always get what we want. We may *want to want* something else, but we end up with what we really want. An easy way to see what you want most is to notice what you're thinking and doing most of the time. That's what you really want. Mystery solved.

Do you desire fear and misery? That's absolutely available. Success in business? Success in love? A forty-year prison sentence? Step right up and make your requests. I'm not talking about mind-based talk-to-yourself-in-the-mirror manifestation here. I'm talking about ordinary manifestation, which means time, attention, and work.

Believe it or not, pull together a hammer, a few nails, a bit of wood, a saw, and a reasonably strong arm, and you can manifest a rough picnic table in about an hour. It's not instant or magical, but it's a sure thing. You can also stay in bed and mind-meld about a picnic table and one may fall off a truck out front. But I wouldn't bet on it.

The way Awakening works is that we get a blast of grace—even The Living Method is simply a vehicle for grace. After that initial blast, what more we get is chiefly the result of what we do. I am talking daily, practical effort and experience here, not the trap of dog-chase-tail, nothing-to-do, no-one-to-do-it, straight jacket of nondual pseudo-philosophy. For most people, that philosophy is a mental evasion that leads away from the Truth.

Betsy and I looked at our savings tonight and beamed like a pair of proud parents. We're two old drunks who were bound for destitution and death but who somehow, through a combination of grace, attention, willingness, and work managed to find ourselves sober. Then, in just a few years of thrifty living and long hours of working at two jobs each, we have manifested a savings account with something in front of the zeroes that isn't a zero. Snap! All it took was all we had. For a long time. That's all abiding, embodied awakening takes, too. And it won't take anything less.

Spiritual understanding works in a far less magical way than we want to think. It's mostly up to us. Don't you hate that? Don't you want it just handed to you? If you don't, you're the rare commodity. We should talk!

Even if your *attention* is on your spirituality, what's your *intention*? Is it to do whatever it takes in order to be a servant of awakening, or is awakening something to master for your personal purposes? If we're still hoping to acquire enlightenment for the benefit of ego, that's going to cloud our intent. If we maintain that position, it's going to kill it. It's an understandable and forgivable, almost impossible-to-resist early phase (yes, I am guilty too), but it's not the direction we want to remain moving in.

If after an initial awakening I continue to strategize about what I'm going to do with "my enlightenment" so that Fred can get a payoff, I better find a way off of that trail, or I have already lost. With that attitude, I am declaring to those of the world who can hear these things that Awakeness is no longer functioning through this body, that I want what I want, and God can take a hike.

Integrity of intent will direct us toward doing whatever it takes to achieve and accept higher levels of reality—for the right reason. And there is only one right reason: for the purposes of IT. Consider the depersonalization of "our" apparent awakening an offering, a Lent-style sacrifice.

If you want to awaken more than you want to sleep, you will wake up. You can't not. If you want to stay awake more than you want to sleep, you'll stay awake. I like to say that I need 51% cooperation if I'm going to be successful at inducing an awakening through someone. If I have 50% cooperation, and it's a good day, I may be able to pull a client over to the clear side. But in the cases where 51% of you wants to stay asleep—sweet dreams. I can't budge you.

This goes for your first awakening or an apparent "reawakening" after a period of reidentification with the body. Your level of cooperation—your integrity of intent—is what helps or prevents your being awake to this arising in this moment. And that moment-by-moment Awakeness is the only thing that counts.

If I want abiding enlightenment more than anything else, then at least 51% of my authentic attention is going to have to be on that process, or I'm going to get what I really want instead: success in love or business, a low golf handicap, or an arrest record. I may declare that I want to be awake more than anything, but if I'm putting 90% of my waking hours into something other than that, does that declaration really hold water?

If you happen to blunder your way to this teaching through all of the worldly and spiritual mazes, the odds are wonderful that I can help you wake up in about two hours, whether it's for your first time or your last time. I'm game. Let's go!

But if you're simply interested in transferring your long-running "poor me/why me" victim story over to the spiritual realm, I'm not the guy to ask for help. After all, it's my job to tell you the truth, to tell you what you need to hear instead of what you want to hear. And I do.

So what have you got your eye on? You better like it.

EIGHTEEN

ONE WITHOUT A SECOND

The Awakeness that is our true nature is experienced as the expansiveness of pure Being. I am referring here to a verb, or verbness, not a noun, so it might be less confusing to say "Beingness." After his awakening, the Buddha was asked if he was now a god, demon or man. We are told the Buddha stated simply, "I am awake."

I say, "I am Awakeness."

When the final tether drops away, even I Am becomes too much. Only Amness remains: brilliant, self-lit, a symphonic "*Aliving*" beyond time, space, judgment or limitation. This *Aliving* is what we are. It knows itself and only itself because there is nothing else for it to know.

Since this *Aliving* is the one thing going on, the ONE without a second, it is not self-reflective. It knows that it is, but it has no idea what it is. It sees only itself and harbors no preferences, allowing What Is to play out upon its screenness. Who, what, when, where, why and how—the fundamental questions of relativity—can only arise from a center, and there is neither center nor edge to boundlessness itself. It has no inside or outside, apex or nadir, beginning or end. This wholeness simply is. It exists. Nothing further can be said about it, although we are going to give it a mighty try.

Opposites are always, always of the dream; they apply only within relativity, which is another word for the dream, meaning our personal world. Opposites are the chief mechanism of the dream. Whatever exists within relativity has an opposite, even if it's an imagined opposite that is not and cannot be fundamentally real. Opposites can, however, certainly appear to be real, and that's good enough for us. Real or not, relativity is our everyday experience, and we should not try to transcend our daily experience with beliefs and philosophy. Neither beliefs nor philosophy fill us up when we are hungry.

Nonduality does not reject relativity—it cannot reject relativity. Nonduality rejects nothing; rather it encompasses everything, including all objects whether they are apparently material or apparently mental. It also includes the conceptual absolute of Beingness, as I use it here. The concepts of absolute and relative are the final bastions of an inferred duality, but because they are opposite concepts, they can only refer to the dream. So for our purposes here, it is closer to the truth to say that they are two different views of the not-two Reality—the Reality that includes them both.

Reality and Nonduality are used here as synonyms, and they are always, always inclusive, never exclusive. Oneness or Beingness suggests the whole potato: there can be nothing other than it and nothing beyond it. There is no other, there is no beyond. What Is rules itself. Relativity is more like french fries, the one potato appearing as many things. However, comparing the one potato with the fries happens only in dreamland.

The *Aliving* that we are is without comparison, for one would have to step outside of the one thing in order to compare the one thing. There is nothing prior to, beyond, or outside of Beingness; the one-without-a-second has no past or future tense and knows no other than itself. There is only Now, which includes whatever is currently arising.

Since aliveness only knows that it is and not what it is, it has no resistance to itself when that self is expressed as arisings. All resistance is the product of an imaginary center, the ego's job until it isn't.

Again, this *Aliving* exists without companion or comparison. This is why we sometimes say it is all-accepting or that it is acceptance itself—because *Aliving* has no alternatives to What Is, as it is, right now. Any complaint or compliance on our part is merely relativity's apparent reaction to the absolute's current expression of Beingness. What Is, above all, is clean. Simple and stripped. Naked and neutral.

However, human beings are not creatures to be held back by mere facts. We have ideas that we like better than truth, simply because those ideas are what allow us to seem to exist. We are fictitious separate beings within a make-believe foreign being, nothing more than ghosts who want to live!

Thus we habitually override our actual experience and defer to our imagination. Until we awaken, we hardly ever live in What Is. We blindly choose to live in what isn't, and so long as we do, we will suffer at the hands of our own imagination. We will get to be right, but we will not get to be free. We can't be both things at the same time.

After awakening, we almost always try to hold onto both of our lovers—truth and fiction. Thus we experience a sense of oscillation, but ultimately we will have to declare ourselves faithful to one or the other. This post-awakening movement is almost always touch and go. Ironically, it's quite difficult to give up nothing in exchange for everything because to so feels like just the other way around! We feel we are giving up everything to get nothing.

Humans are positively addicted to their sense of a separate self, and like all addicts, we live in denial. We deny and defend, unwilling to see-be the truth because living in the truth requires giving up of our imagined autonomy and delicious specialness. But let me be clear: there's nothing wrong with that until an imaginary separate self thinks there is.

We pretend to be a human *this* in search of a cosmic *That*. In fact we are the cosmic *That*, caught helplessly in the pull of our own dream, always being tugged toward self-recognition, clarity, stability, and finally abiding, embodied Awakeness. We pretend to be in bondage so that we can pretend to be set free. Hide. Seek. Find. Celebration!

And so it goes until it doesn't, and the moment comes when the apparent you can, like the Buddha, say "I am awake." Or like I say, "I am Awake*ness.*"

NINETEEN

A SPIRITUAL TEACHER NAMED WILLY

These days our spiritual teacher is an eighteen-pound Tibetan Lama named Willy. He is a two-year-old Lhasa Apso that exploded into our lives fourteen months ago to show us close up what a life lived in abiding enlightenment really looks like. He has done precisely that and has taken our hearts in the process. I would say "stolen," but the truth is that we have given our hearts over to him freely and spontaneously without his ever asking us to do so. We could not fail to love such a radiant spirit.

Traditionally, Lhasa Apsos were the guardians of Tibetan monasteries. Their job was to alert the monks and huge Mastiffs to the presence of outside intruders. I hear they did a really good job, and delivery men to my house would hasten to agree. From what I have seen, however, in between thwarting attacks and burglaries, these fierce guardians probably spent a lot of time in lama laps and holy kitchens begging scraps from the cook. Everyone needs some time off.

Legend has it that when a resident monk died, his soul went to live in one of the monastery's Lhasa Apsos. Something like that is clearly the case with Willy, and it appears that he has gotten himself a real lulu of a house-guest, not just a Lama, but a former Dalai Lama or something. You don't get much spiritually clearer than Willy.

Willy is naturally comfortable in the present moment and needs zero adjustment time between changing events, locales, or laps. Whoever is around is a prize, and whatever is happening is absolutely wonderful. He never met anyone he didn't love, although he does seem adverse to my sister-in-law's cowboy boots. Maybe they're someone he knew in his previous life.

What Is works for Willy, no matter what form it's taking, provided that form is not a possum. Even the clearest of us have our personal challenges, and possums are Willy's. Nonetheless, his experience of a possum is lived out vertically rather than horizontally. The beast is seen and challenged, there is a flash of teeth and the sound of a bark, but the beast is not actually attacked.

Once either the possum or Willy has been removed from the field of near-battle, Willy is content to let bygones be bygones and quickly forgets all about the encounter. I confess, however, that I have upon occasion found him sniffing at the trail of a formerly adversarial marsupial as though he was planning to hunt him down. I get it. I've been known to exhibit that sort of behavior myself. I'm all for making a big show of bravery once the coast is actually clear.

Willy has got meditation down pat. That dog can sit for hours and never complain about either his knees or his obsessions. He puts me to shame in both departments, but I can still soundly beat him out in the spiritual inquiry department, because Willy has no questions! He takes everything just is as it is, and he wastes no time longing for or fretting about imaginary alternatives. He knows that in the end there is just This. THIS This!

In that same way, Willy never asks if he's enlightened, or if he should be, or if he used to be, or if he will be again. He simply lives fully as whatever it is that he is without looking for either imperfection or lack in himself or in the world. Willy knows that What Is represents the culmination of all that has ever been. There's no understanding it, so he doesn't try.

Willy has never once asked, "Why me?" in regard to his having been locked away as a child in a kill shelter, through no fault of his own, and given just seventy-two hours to either raise bail or die. I wasn't there, but I'm willing to bet that he was living every second to its fullest while he was in the slammer. He wasn't waiting for anything. And, of course, someone came to his aid before the clock wore down, finding great joy by bringing great joy.

Willy has never wanted to know why such a cute, sweet, innocent little dog such as him had such a hard lot early in life. The vet said that he'd been treated kindly but had come from a disadvantaged home, meaning his owners had more love than money. When he first took over our house he was more than a mite skinny, had worms, a bald spot on his back, and no hair on his belly due to malnutrition. Yet he was as happy and grateful as he could be, because he was not comparing his lot or his life to anyone else's.

If I had to use just one word to describe Willy, that word could only be Love. That Love's expression are the Joy and Gratitude that erupt spontaneously and volcanically all day and all night. Even in its sleep that little body stretches and rolls, clearly intoxicated with the luxury of simply being alive, of simply having a body when nothing at all was due him.

Scratch his haunches, and Willy will strain upward to lick you in thanks. Kiss him and he will kiss you back—mind the tongue. Throw a stick and he will chase it joyfully. He's not very good at bringing it back, but he is a marvelous chaser. Willy plays to his strengths.

So, can animals help to clear us up spiritually? Can they show us how to live in loving clarity on an ongoing basis? You bet they can! And do. In fact, they will automatically do so if we don't resist them. Kind of like enlightenment. We have to want truth more than we do our victim story. If we do, then we will surely find it. We can't not.

Over the past ten years, my two cats Henry and Dickens, have changed my whole outlook on and experience of the world. My guardian angel, Miss Betsy, mother and best friend to all of us, has given us a model of Goodness to admire and emulate. She has shown us Love in action.

And Willy? Oh my. His is one of the Hundred Thousand Names of God.

TWENTY

PLAYING THE HAND WE ARE DEALT

Life is sort of like a weird game of poker. First we're dealt an initial hand, but we're never happy with what we get. Everyone's got a better hand than we do, except for the ones who don't, but those folks had it coming, or don't know any better, or are somehow better equipped to suffer than we are. Whatever, they don't really count. Thus we don't bother to count them when we frame an opinion about our own cards.

Right from go we know that our cards suck. This much is clear. And many, many people have a better, even far better hand than we do. In fact, it looks like they may have been dealt the hands we rightfully should have gotten! Life is not fair, or just, or good, simply because it's not tilted entirely towards us.

Because we all want what we want when we want it, the want we don't get is quickly converted into a need. So, there it is: we don't have what we need. This is our constant mental field. We didn't have what we needed yesterday, we don't have what we need today, and tomorrow—oh God, we shudder to even think of it. Deprivation and disaster are right around the corner.

Although it's painful to project the future—our precious future—we think about it anyway, and we think about it almost all the time. We obsess. Poor us, damn it.

Why me?
Why these cards?
Why not?

The core benefit of not having what we think we need—measured with our personal ruler, of course—is that we get to develop a victim story, which becomes our most valued asset. Hurrah! I've seen people back directly away from enlightenment—successfully dodge the oncoming bullet of freedom—because they wouldn't be able to hang onto their story if they accepted the invitation of realization. In such cases we already have what we want, but we enjoy making noise about needing something else to complete our story. We actually love living in the mental state of lack.

So, even though we think we have a bad hand of cards, we want to safely sit out of the betting, fearful that we might lose what we have. Yet we want in some mystical Las Vegas sort of way to have the same shot at the pot that the actual players have. Good luck with that.

In Life's poker game, we get to keep drawing new cards every time it's our turn, but of course, we don't have any choice in what the top card in the deck will be and worse yet, we don't have any choice in what card will be magically discarded from our current hand! If so, what choice *do* we have? Our moment of pregnant choice is when we first flip up our draw card, and it all boils down to this: Will we take delivery of it? That is the question that really matters. Will we rest our attention on that next arising? Will we believe it, question it, pursue it, or pass on it?

Arisings arise. Thoughts occur. What we see when we look at them is entirely dependent upon where we're seeing them from. If we're looking from self-interest, our apparent choice and its consequences will be directed by it. The same is true if we're looking from Self-interest, that is, an interest in our *real* Self.

Once there is a spiritual awakening, once the embers of true liberation begin to glow, we are granted the first true choice we ever get: deciding where we will view the world—our deck of arising cards—from. Our personal intent is not doing the actual dealing, but it certainly is the interpreter of all that we receive.

And truth be told, our intent does, in fact, influence the top card. Once it's seen that this is all a dream, a lot of apparent impossibilities are revealed to be possible after all. Simple observing affects the dream in a measurable way. If you don't believe me, fine, go talk to the physicists. Let them take your head where your heart cannot yet go.

Our current experiencing is always composed of trace elements found in the five cards we have deemed the most important over the course of the hand. The ones we have devoted our time and attention to will eventually become what the other players see turned up on the table. We are the fruit of our own tree—directly related, but in no way limited to the roots which initially bore us.

We do not get a direct vote in life. Nonetheless, these units develop a cumulative momentum that is overwhelmingly powerful. It will knock down anything in its way. This is why it is said that the most important quality in a spiritual journey is earnestness, or intention. It's not just about the power of persistence: our attention actually influences the direction of the journey itself. What cards in our hand do we give our magical attention?

The world rises to meet whoever we are—be that mortal man or Eternal Awareness. Ultimately our current experiencing reflects the Divine Attention as it has been affirmed and influenced by and through our human attention and intentions. This is actually beyond cause and effect; it's more subtle than that, and far more spontaneously alive. At the higher levels of spirituality, cause and effect are synonyms.

These units and their experiencing of the world are like living memorials to our past attention. Daily we sculpt our own monuments with the thoughts we allow to lead us. Our "common, ordinary, everyday" attention is more important than most of us can bear to know. These units and their worlds are constantly changing as we draw, retain, reject, or embrace the card deck's latest offering, which is always this arising, in this moment, at this time, in this place.

You must pay attention to your cards. If you retreat from the game, if you refuse to make a bet, you lose the chance to win the pot. As ever, the bottom line is, are we willing to be awake right now? That lazy, retirement brand of enlightenment you've been looking and waiting for? Good luck with that.

TWENTY-ONE

WORKING WITH OUR SECRET TEACHER

Our secret teacher is our own *inner* teacher, what the Hindus call *sat-guru*, or *sad-guru*. Each of us has one. It's a permanent resident, and it's always working for us, but we're usually creating too much noise to hear it. Those who do extensive meditation may very well discover this teacher prior to awakening. However, for the slugs like me, even though I did some serious meditation along the way, discerning the inner teacher may not happen for quite some time, even if we have had an awakening experience.

In my case, I can look back and see my inner teacher at work at a number of critical junctures. Each of these instances created a break in the chain of logic by which I lived my life and helped me narrowly avert disaster. I don't want to imply that the first five decades of my life were logical: those years were chaotic. Yet whatever mad scheme I was engaged in always seemed logical to me.

In those desperate times to which I refer, it would be more accurate to say that my sat-guru forcefully overruled me rather than whispering sweetly. For most of my life, whether I studied and meditated or didn't, I did not have had the presence of mind to notice anything more subtle in the way of life guidance than a sledge hammer blow. If you look back, perhaps you can spot a few of your own moments of guidance, whether subtle or forceful.

These moments of guidance are tremendously helpful, even if we are not aware of being guided, but once you tune into your inner teacher, the benefits start to escalate.

What I'm talking about is consciously and knowingly hearing, feeling, dreaming, or otherwise sensing direction. I first began to take notice of my inner teacher in December of 2009. It had been just over three years since my initial large awakening and precisely two since my second.

From the first day of my awakening, my tortured thoughts had begun to diminish in frequency and volume. In that quieter environment, the nattering voice in my head that I had long mistaken for my inner teacher was slowly revealed as not only a charlatan, but a damn fool as well. First, it would get me in trouble and then I'd turn back to it to get me out. When we're unconscious, it's almost impossible for us to spot our unskillful life patterns that everyone else in the world has long been either weeping over or guffawing about.

I first began to consciously notice the Inner Teacher's direction in little things. I noticed that my resentment toward the large Golden Retriever who seemed to be making his home in the small doorway to my kitchen could only be caused by my believing the thought that it was my world and not his, not even a shared world which we both inhabited.

My reactions were coming from a "me," a me that I already knew full well was false. The unit was simply dancing out its conditioning—as all units must—and my Inner Teacher was quietly giving me the opportunity to shorten that torturous dance by making me consciously aware of what the problem really was—me.

Once I could truly see that the mistake was in my thinking and not the dog's behavior, my resentment dropped like a stone in a well. It took me a couple of times of going through the pattern of getting annoyed and seeing the annoyance arise, but once I did, it was cooked. That pattern went away and has never returned. The dog obstructing the kitchen door no longer gets my goat. I call this process seeing through the pattern.

These days I don't have a fixed habit of meditation or any other practice, but my inner teacher will allow me to see when my thinking is beginning to turn serious. I don't mean that we need to laugh all the time, although veteran video viewers will know that I laugh a lot. What I mean is that I'm fully capable of starting to take myself seriously, and that's always an error. The teaching that flows through this husk has almost nothing to do with Fredness, I promise you. If I take Fredness seriously, suffering arises.

Not taking myself seriously doesn't mean not taking others seriously or ignoring the gravity of the current arising, whether it's the mounting dust in my house or an earthquake in a village in China. It doesn't mean that at all. It means approaching these things thoughtfully, carefully, responsibly, but never with the idea that I'm looking at an actual problem. Enlightenment doesn't make us blind, stupid, or ineffective. On the contrary, it makes us more discerning, wiser, and far more skillful.

When my thinking gets serious about Fredness's life situation—money, business, relationship—or perhaps just cloudy or gloomy for the hell of it, I sit. My inner teacher doesn't throw me in the chair, it simply whispers something telling like, "You recognize that all of these issues are really high quality problems for a guy who should have died drunk in a park years ago, do you not?" I see the error, experience instant gratitude for things exactly as they are, and then sit and marinate in that glow. I make myself available to my Inner Teacher.

I could be in great spirits as I walk to my mailbox, only to find a bill from the IRS for $5,000, and immediately go into misidentification. But as sure as I did, I can virtually guarantee that my inner teacher would offer up in a soft voice, "You're suffering." I've worked with adverse conditions so many times that even in an extreme case like that, I'm pretty sure I'd respond to that warning by immediately seeing through the story, and dropping the "me," thus dropping the suffering. I'd then come inside and take prudent action: call the IRS, hunt up records, or do whatever made sense at the time.

Enlightenment doesn't mean we're incapable of slipping back into believing our thoughts. It means that we don't have to stay there. With enlightenment we are granted the first real choice we've ever had: Where to view the world from. I can view the world from the eyes of God or from the eyes of Fredness, and the world will rise to reach whichever one is looking. It's a weird truth, but it's a truth nonetheless.

I remember talking to Adyashanti about my inner teacher back in the spring of 2010, just as it was beginning to come online on a regular basis and in a clear way. I called it the "Explainer," which he thought was hilarious. All I could report was that I was seeing a great many things in a whole new way and that it clearly wasn't "me" that was causing this. The voice wasn't actually audible, but it was unmistakable. He helpfully clued me in to what was going on, just as I'm doing with you. It's funny how the yin-yang turns round and round.

The best advice I can give you is to learn to listen. If you don't already have a meditation practice, why not take one up, even if it's only for ten minutes a day? It won't kill you and it could really be a big boon. Try unmeditation:

1) Sit comfortably; no specific posture or cushion is required.
2) Close your eyes.
3) Listen.

Be alert to the current arising. If noticing the aliveness of your inner body helps hold you in alertness, do that. But don't do anything else. Don't try to get somewhere else. Don't wait for another state to appear. Sit without expectation, and as much as possible, sit without purpose. See what happens.

TWENTY-TWO

RUNNING THE SHOW IN POST-AWAKENING

Let's pretend I'm a long-term seeker who has just gotten a good glimpse of my True Nature. It may have been my first or just the latest in a string of glimpses. Let's further say that even though it was brief, it was awesome! Aren't they all? This is one place where size does not matter; glimpses of every size and shape feel great.

So the actual glimpse is over, but I'm still resonating with it, maybe still glowing from it, still feeling deeply intimate with Truth, and I know I'll never be quite able to unsee it. Regardless, I'd like another hit, please. Right away. Now, in fact. And God, in case you've misunderstood your directions, go ahead and give me the full-meal deal and please super-size it. I am hungry for more.

The attitude is understandable. These glimpses are so intoxicating, so utterly seductive. It's like I got a little shot of heaven, which is actually pretty much the truth! And then I got dropped back to earth, an earth that is increasingly uncomfortable. Damn it, I had heaven within my reach, almost within my grasp, and then it slipped away, like a silent ship leaving port with me stuck standing on the pier. Heaven is no longer here. Poof!

And earth? Well, just between the two of us, I have to say it just ain't what it used to be. This place is beginning to feel more and more like, well...how else to put it? Hell. That's the word.

I thought that a glimpse of my true nature would make me feel better. And it did. For a while it made me feel a lot better. But now? Not so much. The more Awakeness I experience, the more I suffer when I play make believe that I'm away from it. I have developed quite a taste for the One Taste.

However, I still like being right. I still like knowing the way things should be. I still cherish my precious victim story. So what do I do?

I only get this question about six times a week.

I call it reseeking. I did my fair share of it—it felt like a hell of a lot more than my fair share—even after my rather showy awakening in 2006. I didn't have a teacher to guide me, and at that time there were few books or other resources mentioning post-awakening, and that absence suggested that I should expect an easy one-shot-deal.

What I wanted was the Big Score, in much the same way that lottery buyers want the Big Score. Now, people do win the Powerball Lottery, but U.S. News & World Report states that the odds of any single ticket taking it are 1 in 175,223,510. In other words, we have roughly the same chance of winning whether we do or do not bother to buy a ticket.

My odds of having a beautiful one-shot no-maintenance enlightenment were about the same and so are yours. Recently, I had a Clarity Session with a client who had woken up with me the week prior, and while she was not yet back in the full sleep state, let us say that a lot of clouds had moved in on her between our talks. Oddly enough, however, there was a still a lot of Awakeness functioning as well.

She told me, "It shouldn't be so much work to remain consciously awake."

I get that completely. I felt the same way. I was wrong and so is she. Like me, she will find out that after awakening, we still face a lot of work, a lot of conscious, deliberate, maddening mechanic-ing until we become stable.

We can fight where we are and be bitter at the ridiculously slow pace at which Awakeness is working to colonize the body, and maybe never become conscious again. Sometimes that's actually ego's secret plan. It works, if that's what you want. Zzzzzzzzzzzzzzzzz.... I get to stay right where I am while claiming I want to be somewhere else.

Perfect.

By being opposed to the way Reality is playing out for us in the post-awakening period, we suffer twice over: first from the panic over our sense of dwindling clarity and second from our resistance to how things actually are. Panic and resistance sow the seed for a further reduction in clarity. And on and on. It's a downward spiral that leads to total unconsciousness. I know this because I have experienced complete unconsciousness in post-awakening. It's no fun, and I hope I can help my client avoid the experience.

Our "feeling" that the post-event process of awakening "should be" happening other than the way it is happening is just a dressed up wish, a childish fantasy we're trying to rationalize. It's our argument with God, and it will keep us sleeping soundly for just so long as the argument runs.

I wanted a nice, lazy, sort of blissful, hallucinatory, awakened life—hopefully continuously orgasmic—and where I wouldn't have to remain *alert*, for God's sake. I mean, I didn't want any sort of Awakeness where I had to be responsible; no siree! I wanted it all done *for* me—right now—just like I always wanted everything else. Hop to it, God!

I can want what I want, but I'm still going to get what I get.

Today I have a generally lovely, often blissful life experience as Awakeness. I do not have to do any mechanic-ing. I still have to remain alert to the present arising, but alertness is now built in. It's effortless. It's my natural state, so to speak.

We call this abidance. Betsy and I talked about it recently. It's indescribable. It's delicious. Yet from the outside looking in, it's apparently as ordinary as can be! The extraordinary ordinary. It can't get any better than this. Until tomorrow, when there is further opening.

Nonetheless, it is not continuously orgasmic. Everything in the relative world does not go Fredness's way, but fortunately I have learned that Fredness's opinion doesn't count for much. After all, neither Fredness nor I—or my recently awakened client, for that matter—get a vote on this planet. It feels like it's a voting sort of planet, but it's not.

I can adjust or I can suffer. This body lives in space and time, and therefore, even though I am perfectly aware that there is no space and time, I can state that it takes time for the unit to adjust. Just because I wake up to the dream doesn't mean that either Fredness or even I control it. Fredness would like to control it, but me? No thanks, it's just too good like it is. Amazing how it all works out on its own.

We can be right, or we can be free, but we can't be both at the same time.

I choose freedom. Over and over and over again I choose freedom. Every day, every moment, I choose freedom.

How about you? It's all about right now.

TWENTY-THREE

THE WREN'S STORY

Our front porch has four hanging baskets on it. Within one of them, amid the geraniums, the dusty miller, and the flowing vine whose name I can't remember but which is growing long and green and lovely despite its anonymity, a little Carolina wren has made her home.

The basket is placed so that it is just inches from the glass of the living room window. I sit in that room every morning, drinking hot black tea and reading books about awareness. My chair is about ten feet from the window and is aimed directly at it. I really, really want to tell you the story about how I noticed that wren from the first flit of its tail. I want to tell you how I watched that little bird build her nest from the first day to the last.

But I can't.

Honesty prevails here, which includes owning up to my own inattentiveness to the Life I spend most of my day talking and writing about. I noticed that nest instantly—right after hearing Betsy's excited announcement: "Look, Honey! A wren is building a nest on our porch!"

We're all doing the best we can here. Even me. Betsy doesn't read books on awareness. She doesn't need to. As Byron Katie says, "I know you're either ahead of me, or you'll catch up!" Betsy and I seem to trade those positions back and forth. Like a pair of mountain climbers, one pulls the other up and then the other does the same, and it looks like we are two harmonious beings moving up and down and sideways but forever hooked to the same rope. To put it closer to the truth, there is just a single one of us, apparently divided into yin and yang, constantly circling each other, trading positions, first this way, then that. Each extreme bears the seed of the other extreme.

Once everyone and everything is seen to be absolutely equal, there is no such thing as "higher ground." We are not just on a perfectly even playing field; we are, in fact, the very ground of perfectly even playing.

Thankfully, Momma Wren was not quite finished with her carpentry, so I did get to pay attention to what was going on after I'd been told to. Sometimes that's the best we can muster, is it not? When that's the case, let's try to make it our practice to heed skillful advice as early as we can. So, once I knew she was there, I began to take a serious interest in the wren's affairs. I did watch her patiently bring sticks and straw and build up from the makeshift structure Betsy originally discovered.

Momma Wren was cheerful and diligent, rain or shine. She consistently put the one thing she values most highly into the making of it: her attention. By the time she was done, even I couldn't have missed the fine result of her industriousness. I water those plants manually with a wand, and I can report a seriously obvious and involved lump right in the middle of the plant group. The lump is full of baby wrens now.

That Carolina wren has been being my teacher. (And because what she has taught me is now part of me, she will always be my teacher, can't not be my teacher, whether she's on the porch or it's ten years from now and she's passed on and is apparently a "different part" of Nature, a different form in the field of Life.

After all, teaching, like enlightenment, is all about right now.

If Momma Wren happened to be a talking bird with an average human being's point of view, and you asked her what had transpired in the last few weeks, she would tell you something like this:

"Oh, it's just been terribly difficult! I flew and flew and flew, looking all over the place for a safe place to raise my babies. It's a dangerous world these days, you know. Finally I found a nice snug spot, out of the rain, adequate sun, a windbreak right behind it—oh, just right I tell you! And then, then for God's sake—can you even believe this?—just about the time I get some eggs in there, along comes this monster dumping water on the thing!

"I go to all the trouble to find a spot out of the rain and then he louses it up! I can't say that what he did was directed at me personally, but neither can I say it wasn't. It's suspicious, I know that. He's all over the place with that wretched can of his, wreaking havoc with every stop! You'd think he'd have better things to do.

"And then there's my husband! Mate for life, we wrens do. We're bonded, for God's sake! Yet he refuses to carry his own weight. Get this: I've laid every egg we've ever had! Can you imagine? Every single egg. Then he makes a big show out of helping "build the nest" and "guard the nest" and "feed the children." Rot. There's nothing to all that. But him lay an egg? Never on your life."

99

Fortunately the wren in question is not a talking bird, and she does not show human qualities. As a result, what the wren does is her job. And she doesn't make a fuss about it. She's content to do her job as it morphs: now scouting, now building, now laying, now raising, and finally resting until the cycle begins again. It comes around three times a year for wrens, somewhat less often for humans.

The first question many people will ask after reading this little analogy is, "But is the wren happy?" This question only arises when the bird is seen to be the center of the world. It implies that the happiness of the wren is more important than the babies. Babies are seen to be adjuncts to the central figure, the starring figure, namely us in the guise of a wren.

"Is the wren happy?" implies that the purpose of the world is to make the wren happy. So the wren is not a tool within and for Life, but rather Life is a tool outside of and for the wren. That is the clear implication for the wren, and it is the same for us. The health and balance and simple beingness of the yard and neighborhood is, on a relative level, more important than any single wren, even if it's Poppa Wren and his name is Fred. On an absolute level it must be seen and accepted (but only if we're looking for peace) that, hello-hello, IT'S NOT ABOUT THE WREN!

From the standpoint of nature everything has a job to do. It may be to raise babies, or to be eaten by a cat. Three years ago I had a wren's nest on the same porch, in a similar basket. She had babies, too. We were so excited. And when they morphed into ants in the course of a hot summer day, I took it personally. I could see it was not supposed to be like that. I had a pre-conceived storyline, and Life wasn't following it.

I suffered. But I didn't suffer because something bad happened to the little baby birds. I suffered because something bad happened to me! I didn't get what I wanted. My projections didn't turn out. My future-event storyline was broken. My expectations went unmet. Life was seen to be lacking. I got into an argument with reality and reality won, just as it will at every turn. "But only 100% of the time," as Byron Katie would say so sweetly.

So far as I know, the pair of wrens from three years ago was not admitted to any crisis hospital. I never noticed a line of counselors or mourners. What's to counsel? Life is as it is. What's to mourn? Everything changes, but nothing is ever gained or lost. Life is as it is. Always.

At every moment I can choose to see what is through the limitless eyes of Life Itself, or the extraordinarily limited and necessarily self-centered eyes of an individual. In the first instance I will be free. Maybe happy or maybe not so happy but always free. Peace is beyond the happiness I'm speaking of, which is condition-driven. Really I am speaking of joy. Freedom, peace, joy: these are three words which really mean the same thing here. And I cannot have this freedom, nor this peace, nor this joy, until and unless I value truth more than I do comfort.

If I choose comfort, I choose the familiar, a story, but no matter how great or grand or apparently permanent or seemingly special due to its apex of happiness or nadir of horror, I will eventually suffer because of that story. I may fly today, but I will be walking tomorrow and crawling the next day. That's just the way it works. I'm not saying it's bad, or even that it's the wrong choice. I just say, "Let us make these decisions consciously rather than by default."

My resident wren does not have a story. She does what she does without projection, without complaint, without expectation. And that is her teaching: Do your job and shut up about it. Everything is as it is—and all is well.

TWENTY-FOUR

CHARACTER ADDICTION

On the deepest plane, each of us is an archetype for all of us, so to address any single person's issues, questions, progress, or dead-ends will also be beneficial at a macroscopic level. Again and again and again, there is just One thing going on. As a result, I know of no better laboratory culture to study than the one that arises from the Petri dish of this teaching. Let's jump right in.

Call him Bob. I'm not sure what he does for a living, but he's a little like me, an independent-minded entrepreneur-type who's had the good fortune to have made some money along the way, and the far-less-fun fortune of losing a lot of it as well. Money comes and it goes. The one thing you can count on with money is that you can't count on it.

When Bob and I first talked, it was clear that my new friend was suffering from an overdose of Bobness. This is the same thing we're all suffering from: addiction to our characters. They know so much. They're so important. And best of all, they're right. They have the secret lowdown on everybody and everything. Sure they do.

Bob had studied Nonduality for a long time and had a wonderful intellectual understanding of it, but not much that was experiential, which is why he contacted me. I get this a lot. Just this morning a gentleman in Holland asked me to please help him move his knowledge from "his head to his stomach." That says it as well as anything I can come up with. We succeeded, by the way.

Bob's Awakening Session took place via Skype, with him using a tablet computer in a vacant house he owned. He started out as a bit of a tough nut, simply because he "knew" so much. I get a lot of that, too. When you know a lot, it's easy to reference your information instead of your experience. But information won't get you out of the cul de sac

Fortunately I was able to talk Bob into dumbing himself down for our two hours together. When I hit a spot where someone's information is choking out the possibility of their seeing the truth, I'll often tell them, "The one who knows about all of this is not the one who's making progress. The one who knows all of this is the one who's preventing it." The ego can't free the ego. If it could, it would have already done so.

Bob came around beautifully and woke up right on time, meaning he woke up about where I had planned for him to wake up. I never know exactly where someone is going to get it, but it's usually somewhere in a particular 15-minute span that occurs in every session. At any rate, Bob woke up very clearly. He came to know/see/be Truth. I tested him a bit, which is also a way of helping the client's experience deepen. He told me flat out that there was no doubt in his mind that what he'd found in our work together was the truth and nothing but the truth. He really got it.

Then came the first Clarity Session. When Bob and I got together the second time, it was quite evident that he was back in deep sleep. And he didn't remember a thing! I've certainly had this happen before, but not very many times, and it never fails to surprise me when they remember nothing. Had someone been watching our second session, they might very well have thought that Bob and I'd never even met before, much less shared the intimate secrets of Life together.

This kind of thing was more common earlier in my teaching, but it seems to be less and less so as I go. I don't get so many spiky angels-and-fireworks explosions as I used to—in fact I haven't seen one in quite a while—but I don't get the yang side of that yin either. When you go up very far very fast, remember that the trip down is likely to happen the same way. The whole process with my clients is much more even now.

On this afternoon I did what I had to do: I woke ole Bob back up. This time, instead of taking two hours, it took about forty-five minutes. That, I pointed out to a once again happy and smiling Bob, was progress. When he woke up that second time, he remembered everything that had occurred the first time. One way of putting this phenomenon into words is to say that the Bob character was absent each time Awakeness came around, and so the Bob character held no memory of the experience.

Memories would have probably arisen later on of their own accord, but who knows? We often say that once you have a Nondual awakening you can't unsee it, and it's usually true, but I've seen eight or ten exceptions. That's out of probably 500 people I've helped wake up since I began my practice, so the odds of its happening are not long, but it can and does happen. But this was the first time I'd ever had someone forget multiple times after multiple meetings. This thing will really screw with your mind, will it not?

Bob and I spent four Sunday afternoons together, and I had to wake him up every single time. I'm laughing as I write this because a case of this kind is not good for my resume, you know? But apparently my job for that month was to wake Bob up several times, and Bob's job, after waking up and chatting with the insight of Buddha himself, was to go back to sleep and forget all about it! You have to hand it to us: we both performed our jobs admirably.

So every week I had to start from scratch and prove myself all over again, and every time he woke back up and then remembered having woken up previously—but not until he was awake again, and then for only as long as conscious Awakeness was flowing through the Bob unit. It was bizarre.

Let me try to be a little more technically clear. Bob never woke up, just like Fred never woke up. In truth, it is always Awakeness that wakes up. I've told this story the way I have, because that's the way that it would have looked to an outside observer, and on anything other than a metaphysical level it would be true. However, in the end, I'm just languaging about a subject which is impossible to language about. So if there feels like a "gap" in any of this, you'll have to cross it intuitively; this is as close as I can come with words.

The good news is that given enough time, even I can spot a pattern. In our last meeting I told Bob, "I don't say this to hurt your feelings. I say this to try and be helpful. Right now you simply like being Bob more than you like being awake."

Bob jumped right on that! He said, "You know, you just might be right!" I so admired that immediate and utter honesty. I was right, and we both knew it.

In the four afternoons we'd spent together, and the one he'd missed without cancellation or apology, I had come to know a very strong-willed character. I mean by that someone who's self-assertive and fond of control. Bob, like all of us, enjoys being right. And there's nothing wrong with indulging yourself in being right if you're not set on living in Awakeness.

Rightness, however, is anathema to awake living. There has to be someone there in order for one to be right. Somebody has to refer to a belief, state an opinion, or take a position. Awakeness only shows up in the absence of that character, never in its presence.

In the end, Bob and I talked about what we'd discovered, and what it likely meant. He was almost ready to live in Awakeness, that much was clear—otherwise he wouldn't have found himself talking to me. But for now, he should enjoy Bobness! Why not? Awakeness is perfectly willing and happy to function unconsciously until it isn't. Bob got a little advance notice about what was coming, that's all.

Is Bob supposed to be living every day in Awakeness? NO. How do we know? HE ISN'T. How will we know when he is supposed to be living every day in Awakeness? HE WILL BE. End of story; it's just that cut and dried. There are no shoulds in What Is.

For my part, I very much enjoyed working with Bobness, and I wouldn't be surprised to see us talking in the future. I remember being quite addicted to my own character. When the character found himself in a legal quagmire that included weekend visits to jail, the addiction to my character fell away quite naturally. And what happened next? I woke up—I'm speaking as Awakeness now.

We are where we are until we're someplace else, and wherever we are at any given moment is just fine. It really is all good.

TWENTY-FIVE

REALITY ON RYE

Some time ago, I met my friend Larry for lunch at a deli. We'd never met in person, but Larry is a regular follower of my website. He consistently leaves comments and sends me personal emails. We've gone back and forth quite a bit. He happens to live in a town near mine, and when he asked me to lunch, I accepted.

When I arrived at the deli, Larry recognized me from my picture on the website and came out to greet me. It's a busy college spot, but he had come early and found a great table tucked away in the back. I love that forethought and that care. This is a man who is preparing the ground ahead of time for a meeting of importance. He is not taking anything for granted; he is attentive. He is opening the window and pulling back the drapes just in case the sun decides to shine. It did.

My friend is somewhere near my age, quite a normal guy, which was great. We could talk about important questions as two ordinary men of earnestness. I had already told Larry via email that I was not much of a small talker, so we started right away to talk about the most important questions of all.

The sun began to noticeably shine (it is always already shining) about forty-five minutes into our time together, which was a total of two hours. It began to shine in response to questions I asked. I asked Larry about his current experience, right then and there. I asked him to test things, to question things, to offer his experience of things as they were right there, at our table, as we were sitting there.

There was no hypothetical talk, no theory, no bullshit. We had already spoken of the paths of monks and mystics, which is all quite interesting, but in the end, who really cares? How about us? Those tales are just interesting stories, but they are someone else's drama. I suggested we take a look at Larry's path: professional, late-life father, husband, householder, seeker, and most importantly, Larry-the-believer-in-specific-things.

He'd sent me an email a few days before that had already tipped me on why he had not seen his Original Face, though he certainly wanted to and had been trying to, and absolutely planned to. He just had a few conditions that God needed to meet first.

Understanding all of that as background, I had come ready to deal with those specific beliefs. I knew that in the absence of those beliefs, the sun would noticeably, automatically be seen to be shining. I would see Myself consciously sitting across the table from Fredness. What I mean by that is that I saw Myself sitting across from me as soon as we sat down. What Larry saw was Fred.

I was seeing Truth. Larry was seeing illusion. There is only One. All I had to do was move my friend from standing as Larryness to standing as Awareness. Not later, right then. Not when he gets a promotion. Not when his child finishes college. Not when the back fence is finished. Right now. Stand as Awareness in this moment. Once that stand has been taken, there's never any unseeing it. Never. We can think we unsee it, we can believe we unsee it, but we don't, we can't. The snake has been seen to be a rope, as the old saying goes.

We can only be Awakeness right now. We can only be Awakeness right here. There's no other time, no other place. We can't wait until we've quieted our minds or until the next book comes in the mail from Amazon. That will never happen. Never. I am not leaving any room to squirm here. NEVER. Awakening is NOW or NEVER.

And then, for Larry, there came The Shift. Gently. No fireworks. The rainbow that had been hiding Divinity from Itself simply disappeared. My teacher gave me this rainbow metaphor, which I passed along to Larry. Many people use clouds in front of the sun to teach with, and that's fine, that's beautiful; I use that sometimes. But the rainbow is a little more subtle and a little truer because a rainbow is not actually an obstruction; a rainbow doesn't actually exist! If we see a rainbow and we follow it to its end, we find only open air. It's an illusion.

The Dream is just such an illusion. And every excuse we have for not being awake right now is a dream excuse. We are always already awake, but we are claiming obstruction from a rainbow we ourselves have invented! For an hour I talked openly to Myself through the Fred mask and the Larry mask. I-as-we laughed at the absurdity of it, at the wonderful trickery of Me, of maya, of samsara, of illusion. There was tearing up over there at the incredible relief. There was laughter over here at the foolishness I clung to over there, and then mutual laughter when it was seen through and dropped.

107

The good news is that with each new True Seeing our capacity to accept seeing expands. There is no lazy awakeness, which is what so many people want. We have to be attentive: new beliefs and opinions are constantly springing up. We have to be willing to trade in our rightness for complete lostness. Over and over and over. There may be a shorter path for some, but there hasn't been for me.

When Larry paid the lunch tab, he was seeing the truth. Whether or not he is living in the truth at this moment, I don't know, but I can tell you that he knows the truth. So do you. We don't have to invent anything new. We just have to drop something old. We just have to drop something old and then remember something much, much older.

TWENTY-SIX

PRACTICING TO BE YOU

Whenever I speak of any "practice," let me clear about what I mean. I am always, always speaking of You, simply but consciously practicing being You. You may be using the Susan or Robert units to do it through, but it's still just You consciously practicing being You. It can't be any other way.

So, we are never doing a practice for the purpose of getting good at the mindful mechanism itself, be it meditation, unmeditation, inquiry, kinhin, singing, chanting, drumming, dancing, japa, mindfulness, or whatever. Who cares if we have gotten really good at looking and feeling spiritual in the dream? How about that waking up thing?

And we are not practicing so that we will wake up clearer later.

There is no "later" that exists anywhere but in the human imagination. There is only Now. So it's now or never. We are clear now or we are not. We are awake to this arising or we are not. We are currently and consciously experiencing ourselves as our Self, or we are not. Conscious Awakeness is what counts, and ultimately it's all that counts. So practice is about our actively engaging the helpful-if-noisy-unit you're wearing so that You can experience Yourself as Yourself through that unit right in this ever-present Nowness.

That's what I mean by practice.

Let us assume that at some point you have known a higher level of clarity which defies description, but not experience. It might have been last night, a week ago, or that wonderful time back in '72 that you just can't get out of your head. Despite that known, certain, first-hand experience of real clarity, at this moment the "little you" which cannot be found, but which You nonetheless generally believe Yourself to be, isn't feeling especially clear and bright. It feels cloudy, and cloudy feels like crap. And then the persistent question arises:

How could this have happened? AGAIN?! Damn it!

In that blessed but now-distant clear moment, by God, just as you were perhaps impatiently prodding the Susan or Robert unit to "Wake up and stay that way!" by some mysterious grace IT descended upon you for a second, a minute, an hour, six months, whatever. Bliss! Relief! Knowing! Rest! Peace! Ahhhh...

Or perhaps you were simply walking to the car—this happened to me once—and it descended unasked, unbegged, unstrived for. Or maybe it comes as a complete surprise if you have not previously been on the path. Bliss! Relief! Knowing! Rest! Peace! Ahhhh...

It was seen to be so incredibly obvious! How could anyone NOT see it? It was all you could do to even get to sleep! Yet a few hours later you woke up bright and early, excited to see the world in this new fashion, and you looked around with an anticipatory grin...and you couldn't see a damn thing. My room. My bed. My feet. Monday. This is the same old reality I USED to have! And it still sucks.

What in the hell is going on here?

Welcome to post-awakening. It is many things, but steady isn't one of them! Some time ago, I had a Clarity Session with a Canadian client who had previously woken up with me. We had barely started when she exclaimed, "It feels like I'm going insane!" I told her, "Yes, it does feel like that, or at least it can, but what's actually happening is that you're going sane instead."

Going sane in an insane world is not a walk in the park. The one good thing is that there won't be a crowd, you can bet on that. Are you feeling like the only onion in the apple barrel? Please. Been there, done that, got the T-shirt.

"I feel raw," my friend told me. Even so, I notice that my friend didn't ask me if I could somehow undo her undoing. We love to bitch about the process, but we are not giving up enlightenment!

Once we reach a certain stage—and my Canadian client is well beyond the turning back point—then like it or not, we're are going on the Big Ride, and it's just a matter of how deep our claw marks will be as we move along the track.

One of the funniest paradoxes in the world is that whether Truth has been seen in a quick glimpse or experienced through a longer-but-never-long-enough awakening that was accompanied by a spiritual experience, what we've seen is that the "little me," in my case Fred, doesn't actually exist. There's no separation, so there's no room for an independent Fred. Regardless, once the brightness appears to have passed, fear once again arises that awakening means losing this seen-to-be-non-existent Fred. I should be so lucky!

That fear, ungrounded or not, talks to us. In fact, it often screams.

The voice in the head is not keen on spirituality. It likes pretending to exist, and it knows a threat when it sees one. Awakening is rarely a lethal threat to an ego, but it is a serious danger to the voice in the head. Granted, the voice in my head is still talking, many years into awakening. But it doesn't talk nearly so loud, and it doesn't talk nearly so often, and when it does talk I find that I have the open choice as to whether I want to listen to it or not. Exercising that choice is a practice.

If you'll notice what the voice is saying, it's really just an unending argument with the world. It knows precisely how things should go, how people should behave, what the weather should be, and on and on and on. Funny thing is, I've noticed that it's never in actual agreement with how things are going. It is the Voice of Resistance to What Is. It is the Voice of Separation.

Waking up may reduce the volume and frequency of the voice. Or, conversely, it may ignite it! I've seen it go either way initially. No matter. If we work at gaining clarity—and greater clarity probably won't come if we don't work at it—then it'll begin to quiet down.

The best way I know of to encourage that quieting down is to simply pay attention to whatever it is that you're doing NOW. That voice is all about the fearful past and the foreboding future. It knows nothing about the present moment. It doesn't even know that now exists! That's because when we're paying attention to what's happening right now, we cannot simultaneously entertain the voice. Paying attention to Now is a practice.

If we're not paying attention to the voice in our head, then it cannot run or ruin our lives. I found out all about this while in recovery from Addiction to Everything. I realized that I don't have to take delivery of every ridiculous thought that comes down the pike. I can pay attention to my body instead. My body is fine, always has been. It's only the mind telling it that it's not fine that's making it experience not-fineness. Paying attention to your body is a practice.

We can only put our attention on one thing at a time. "multi-tasking" is a myth. It's always first this, then that, then the other, no matter how quickly or smoothly we may seem to blend a set of tasks. If your attention is on slicing that apple, or walking to the car, or mowing the lawn, then it cannot—in any given instant—also be screaming about how things are wrong and scary and awful, and thus keep us leashed to the idea of duality. Be mindful of where you are placing your attention.

There is no actual duality. None. It's just a thought that's been believed. Practice mindfulness and notice that you're clearer instantly. It'll work as long as you do.

The great news is that we don't have to wait to start mindfulness practice. We don't need any special clothes, or cushions, or teachers. We don't have to fly anywhere, or call our spouses to get an okay. We can do it to ourselves, by ourselves, and we can do it NOW. Why not try it? Is the voice in your head telling you that you don't need to do it, or that you don't have the time, or providing some other excuse for you?

Notice that the very thing you want to quiet is also the only thing that objects to your simply putting your focus on this very moment. Outside of the voice in your head, can you find any real excuse? I didn't think so.

Be. Here. Now. And pay attention to what you're doing in it!

TWENTY-SEVEN

POSTCARDS FROM THE GONE ROAD

Even if we're awake, we have to live life, and a lot of life seems far from cosmic. So, how does Awakeness manifest itself in the mundane aspects of life, and more pointedly, how does it contribute to flow? No one can predict the next moment, but it sure looks as if clarity can sometimes help us skillfully navigate the sticky issues of everyday life. But don't depend on it! Flow has its own notions of when to cooperate and when not to. Let's explore the subtle interplay of acceptance and action, or at least apparent action, using an example from my life. What can simple noticing achieve?

This morning Betsy and I were talking about weight. When you reach our age, in the 60s, you'll find that putting on weight has become the unit's default position. You don't have to eat more, it'll just not process food in the same way it used to, so weight begins to accrue. Your metabolism slows, all that sort of thing. Middle-age spread. Neither one of us has a serious problem with it, but neither one of us wants it. We've certainly done our share of calorie counting.

A few months ago—three? four?—we both noticed that we were heavier than we were comfortable with either mentally or physically. I'm not talking about active resistance to the weight we already were, but there was a little bell that rang in us suggesting that it was a situation that might bear a bit of attention.

Awakeness is expressing itself as everything-everywhere, the one-thing-only-thing, showing up as here-now. Within that Awakeness, but not other than that, there is

113

attention. Please don't Nondual Police me; I'm speaking plainly here. Essentially attention is the tool by which Awakeness notices itself. It's not separate, but there is a feeling as if it is so. Notice your own attention right now and you'll see what I'm talking about.

As part of the attention we shone on our weight, we talked about it, allowing additional light to play on the issue. We discussed possible health ramifications and how our life together might be even more fun if there was a little less of each of us around to enjoy it! This is not a mystical sort of looking, just a conscious looking. Awakeness happens to be consciously operating through these two arisings. It sees only the truth, and when it does, anything false shows up like pig in a punchbowl.

The lie of, "I'm eating too much, but it doesn't matter because there's really no one to get fat" was clearly seen through by both of us. We didn't even know that yet, but I can see it in reverse. As part of that reverse seeing, I notice that Betsy joined a gym and that she went to work out when she went, but that it was not an everyday thing. It was not a practice. It simply happened spontaneously each time—even if it was on her calendar! She also noticed that she began to simply watch what she was eating. I don't use the word "watch" in the sense of regulating; I use it in the sense of really watching, with honesty and openness. Mindfully. There was no calorie counting, no dark-night-of-the-soul: she just noticed what she ate and when she ate it.

I followed a somewhat different strategy, though I also began to notice what I ate and when I ate it. But early on, when hunger arose, I'd see if I could find an owner of the hunger. I found that when I asked myself if anyone owned the hunger, the answer was always no. When it's clearly seen that there's no owner associated with the thought of hunger (or any other thought for that matter), the hunger often seems to just drop away of it's own accord. The bubble keeps on bubbling up to the top and out of sight if nothing traps it below the surface.

I used to work out with weights, and may again, but I notice I'm not doing it right now. Right now I'm writing a lot and talking to a bunch of people on Skype and tending to this fast-growing teaching practice I've fallen into. I tell myself I don't have the time to work out, but the truth is I don't have as much interest in working out as I do in teaching. I'm putting my attention on my work and not my body. At the moment that seems fairly prudent and reasonable.

This morning Betsy and I were standing in our kitchen talking, both of us glowing like a couple of branding irons, just so happy and alive—and thin, which is astounding because, other than noticing our eating habits and Betsy's moderate exercise program, neither one of us has really done anything to lose weight. For seven days of the week we live at our desks for many hours of the day—nearly all of them in my case. Still, we lost weight.

Betsy's weight has dropped to a level where it hasn't been in years. She's pulling some smaller stuff out of the closet, and she looks like a million bucks and change. My wife does not look 60 years old or even close. My wife looks what she is—timeless. She still has to regularly fend off admiring men. If I didn't already know her, I'd want to know her. I get it.

My weight also has dropped—and stayed—at the lowest point it's been since I was 35 or 40. And I'm not counting calories or doing without. I noticed that I pulled a pint of Ben & Jerry's out of the freezer the other night, put chocolate and nuts on it, and ate the whole bowl. I didn't feel bad about it; rather, I thoroughly enjoyed it. It was great! No guilt, no shame, no worry. The body is always doing what it's doing; it's not actually my job to mentally mind it or scold it. I didn't crave another bowl the next day. A couple of days later, when I stepped on the scale I noticed I was still at 164 and small change. I must have exchanged those Ben and Jerry calories by not eating something else. I don't know. I don't remember. It wasn't a decision.

I can't tell you precisely what's happening, but I can tell you that we've accepted, celebrated, whatever weight we were at every moment, at every pound of the way, including where we were before this strange little program began itself. So, what are we doing and how are we doing it? Can't tell you, don't have a clue. Is it tied to living as Awakeness? Absolutely. Everything these units do these days is "tied to Awakeness". These units are not other than Awakeness. Most of the time, they are living from their true nature, yet within the world. These bodies are windows, not walls.

I was as happy as a wet clam at 177 plus, and I'm tickled to death at 164. I do notice that my clothes fit better and that I'm generally more comfortable at this weight than I was at the former. My doctor would tell me it's healthier. He might be right; I wouldn't bother to argue with him, because I don't know. I can't know that this seemingly strange expression of clarity-at-play-in-the-world-of -weight-loss will last. I can't know that it won't. I don't know much at all. I'm certainly not resistant to its lasting! By the same token, I'm not married to its staying. But I'm going to stick with noticing. Come on bubbles, come on arisings! Have it it! I'm awake to all of you!

I am Awakeness itself. So is Betsy. So are you.

TWENTY-EIGHT

A NARRATIVE FROM NOWHERE

Most people approach the awakening process with some wrongheaded ideas. Three of the big ones are that human beings awaken, that an initial awakening solves all human problems, and that there is nothing more to do after awakening. All these ideas are interrelated and together they create quite a house of cards.

Recently, I was Skyping with a Canadian client, a woman who has woken up a couple of times with me at the wheel—call her Molly. Saying that Molly has previously woken up is, of course, just languaging about what actually happens when awakening occurs. My client never woke up. None of them do. Neither did I. Neither will you.

Awakeness itself is what wakes up, or more accurately Awakeness comes to conscious awareness of itself, but the unit's memory will, in its muddy hindsight, tell our ego that it was an apparent individual who had an "awakening experience." It is almost inevitable, then, that at some point the ego will think that it screwed up and lost its awakening. Back in the dream, ego demands to know how in the hell do I get my awakening back? Well, I'm sorry, but you can't "get back" something you never had, and ego never had squat. Yet for someone on the outside looking in on a session, it would have certainly looked like it was the human client who woke up in our meeting. You have to be sitting in the client's chair or already have conscious Awareness flowing through your unit in order to know what's actually taking place. It ain't what it looks like!

When I met with Molly for our clarity session, I could see that she was terribly frustrated, and she told me in so many words, *I am out cold*. Actually, the fact that she knew she was "out cold" is a clear indicator that she wasn't, but it was close enough. And then she said, "Now, please, you do whatever it is that you do!" She tossed me the hand grenade with a look that seemed to say, "I'm sure the pin is around here somewhere. Good luck!"

I went to work on her and tried several angles—experiments, investigations, and inquiries—with no success. Forty-five minutes into our meeting I saw I was getting nowhere. Now she was not only frustrated, but she was worrying that I wasn't going to be able to help her. So, I had made things worse. Could I perchance make them better?

I wish I could tell you that I have no preference as to whether my clients wake up or not. Wouldn't that be lovely—The Great Unmoved Sage. But I can't tell you that and tell the truth. I care. Maybe I'll graduate to Great Unmoved in another life, but in this one, it matters. Granted, I'm not married to any particular end result, but I certainly have my preference.

I want people to get it if they're supposed to get it. Since I can't know if they're supposed get it or not, I give every single client my very best stuff every single time. With every session, I win or lose my fake little angel wings. If I wake you up, I'm your hero, and you think I'm much wiser and more skillful than I actually am. If I don't, then I'm probably a fraud and should be run out of town. It's harsh, but comes with the territory. It's me who's backing up against the wall and taking on all comers. No one's forcing me. I don't think.

On this day, as I say, nothing was working for Molly. I really didn't know what to do. And I didn't need to. Something popped into my head. "Okay," I said, "try this." Words started coming out of my mouth, and a whole new narrative track arrived and arose spontaneously. Not only was it brand new, but it was nothing I had even thought about before. It came out of nowhere, whole cloth, rough but powerful.

Conscious Awakeness was again flowing through Molly in about fifteen minutes. We talked for another fifteen, and then we parted, both of us tired, both of us happy. Later that night, she sent me an email that showed she was doing fine, still consciously awake.

Is she done? Most likely not.

Molly is now playing the clearing game, which may be played actively, passively, or most often, both ways. Ironically, the clearing aspect of our journey usually comes with a lot of suffering. But why? Why do we have to clear? Why can't we just get it all in one shot?

The best answer is that sudden awakening is not the same thing as sudden complete understanding. At any given point we know what we know, but we don't know what we don't know. Anyone who's had an initial awakening is like a brilliant first-grader. When you move on to second grade, your understanding moves on too. I see teachers backing up on what they've said all the time, particularly those who have early in their careers sworn that there's nothing to do and no one to do it, that nothing is real and therefore nothing matters, and that's the Way of It, and that's the last word.

One of the more famous teachers in Nonduality has in recent times been restating his position on that sort of thing. I admire him for having done it and done it up-front, in public. His short word on the change in his teaching? "My first two books? Not so much." And no, I'm not going to tell you who he is. If you're a close follower, you already know. If you're not, it doesn't matter anyway.

You may counter, didn't Eckhart Tolle and Byron Katie and Ramana Maharshi and Nisargadatta get it all in one whack—complete awakening and complete understanding in one fell swoop? The answer is no, they did not. Eckhart had his years in the park. Katie had her time in the desert, during which she developed The Work as a counter-measure to the madness still patterning through the unit. It was long years between Ramana's initial awakening and the day he began to teach. Any devoted student of Nisargadatta can see a maturing in his teaching as it progresses.

So why should you and I be any different from all these shining examples? Well, typically we are not. I say "typically," because I like to leave the door open to all possibilities, but I know a lot of awake beings, and I don't know a single one who woke up once, got it all, and has now retired in Brightness and gone back to drinking beer and watching football from a fetal position on the couch.

The reason that we drift or jump back into unconsciousness is always the same: ego picks an argument with What Is. It may even win the argument, but it will always do so at the price of freedom. As I love to remind myself, we can be free, or we can be right, but we can't be both at the same time. I have seen Molly absolutely clear as a bell. We have even talked about her possibly becoming someone who can live this Truth well enough to share it in a public way. If so, it'll be a little while yet; I see that now. She needs more clearing.

I know pretty much every misstep that can be taken in the clearing process. I took all of them—more than once. I know very well how long-term thinkers think, what they experience, and the ground they have to cover. Without all of that, The Living Method would never have been birthed through this unit. It takes one to know one, and because I know the seekers' mental map so well, I can essentially trick them into doing what they want to do—come to know their True Nature.

But that does not solve all problems and it is not the finish line.

TWENTY-NINE

WHEN SUFFERING COMES CALLING

One morning a while back my dearest friend suffering was in my bedroom the instant I opened my eyes. This may sound unpleasant, and it is at first, but whenever suffering drops by, it's also the opportunity to discover the truth—if I'm willing to trade in comfort to do so. What happened?

My alarm clock, which I'd suspected to be broken but had been unwilling to replace because I'd held the opinion that it shouldn't be broken, proved itself to undeniably be broken. I had held an opinion: shouldn't. Reality had held a fact: is. Guess who's going to win that argument?

The digital bell was showing up on the display, meaning that I, by God, had done my part. I'd properly set the thing, yet no alarm signal had sounded. I held the traitorous machine in my hand and eyed it with loathing. Although I had insisted on the story "My alarm clock should ring at the time I set it," the alarm clock had opted out of that narrative. In my opinion, it had gone rogue, but a sane person would certainly side with the clock: It wasn't supposed to ring, so it didn't. By contrast, I chose to interpret this impersonal event as evidence that something wrong had happened. I had done my part, but the universe had not. God had dropped the ball.

The facts are simpler than that. I did do my part, and the universe did its part, too. Everything turned out just fine. What I chose to do with those raw facts was completely my business. I could leave them the hell alone, go buy another clock, and surrender to the fact that I was clearly supposed to have gotten up at 9:30 instead of

119

7:00, or I could make up a contrary storyline and suffer. God didn't care which way I wanted to go. I chose to be insane until my dear friend, suffering, forced me into line with sanity.

Whenever I suffer, I know it's time to start noticing, not analyzing, not judging, not blaming, just noticing. I noticed that I was holding onto an opinion: "I got up later than I was supposed to." I noticed that reality was holding a fact: "Fred got up at 9:30." There's no suffering in that fact. There's no problem with that fact. Truly, it is what it is. So, in the face of the truth that hanging onto my storyline would require suffering, I dropped my comfortable righteousness which insisted "I am right in my storyline and when the world contradicts that storyline, IT is wrong."

The world is never wrong. The world is what it is. I can hold opinions that run counter to that. But I have to suffer if I do, so I completely dropped the notion that the alarm clock was broken. On the contrary, it was doing exactly what it was supposed to be doing, which in this fresh new Now was not ringing. I could now absolutely count on it not ringing. Unless, of course, it rang.

I noticed that the thought "I should have gotten up at 7:00 a.m." made me feel stressful. I noticed it reintroduced me to my friend, suffering. I hadn't gotten up at 7:00, so what value was there in hanging onto the lie that I should have? I realized I had been insane. I had thought wrong. In fact, I was supposed to have gotten up at 9:30. Great! I had been right on time! End of suffering.

By the way, lest you think that surrender equates with a lack of action, let me tell you that my alarm clock continues to have the option of not-ringing if it wants to not-ring, but it'll have to live in the freedom of not-ringing within the confines of the city dump, where the trash collectors have no doubt deposited it.

The idea of "7:00 a.m." is a collective myth; I know that. The notion that "alarm clocks should ring when they're set" is another collective myth; I know that, too. Neither one is true unless it is. But that did not keep me from buying a new alarm clock. So far, it has done me the honor of ringing at 7:00 a.m. Who knows about tomorrow morning? It may not. Either way, there's no problem at all.

THIRTY

"Our body is our temple. We should therefore respect it, understanding its importance and always return to it; it is our refuge."

~Thich Nhat Hanh

Call her Lisa. She lives in Florida. I would guess she's in her late 20s or early 30s. Lisa is smart, charming, and has a good sense of humor. We get along really well because we understand each other in a fundamental way. Besides sharing this teaching, we also share a history of successful, long-term, Twelve Step recovery, which among like-minded people can be a very special sort of bond.

In short, we've both been to hell. We're not there now. Hallelujah! Gratitude is not just a good idea for us, it's a way of life. We get it.

Lisa came to know her True Nature with me in an Awakening Session. She had a beautifully clear experience. I still remember the tears that rolled down her cheeks as Truth dawned on her. It was quite moving. I never "get used to it," and I never want to.

Lisa and I had a Clarity Session about three weeks later, and I found her unsettled. She'd backed up into some reidentification with the body, which almost always happens, but which is prone to occur more quickly and more deeply when we find ourselves in both early awakening and turbulent conditions. Lisa's situation met that description, as many do. It's not at all uncommon to find the two paths crossing each other.

Our first Clarity Session went smoothly, but when we said goodbye, I didn't leave with the feeling that I'd been able to really stabilize her. I had done my part, which is all I can ever do, and I had to be content with that. The fruits of my work are none of my business. The willingness and effort are. I play my role with relish.

A few weeks after our second session, I got rather an urgent email asking if I could meet with her again right away. Lisa was experiencing anxiety and depression, something she'd brought up before. She thought it must be tied into her awakening. I was not so sure. I was booked up for a couple of weeks, but I managed to sandwich her in within a couple of days, the way my doctor will agree to see me on short notice if I come down with a nasty virus or something.

Let me be crystal clear: I am absolutely not any kind of therapist or dream-state counselor, but I am an insightful guy who—when asked—is willing to tell people the truth quite directly—even if part of them doesn't want to hear it. That characteristic earns me both great loyalty and occasional enmity. It is what it is. It's what I do.

When the Skype screen opened, Lisa was sitting in the usual place, with her usual bright white T-shirt, but the bright eyes I'd seen before were missing. Lisa looked wrung out. Tired. Worried. After a quick hello, I immediately said, "Before we start into anything else, I want to ask you a plain, non-spiritual question, because I think it's pertinent." She nodded okay.

"Lisa, I remember you mentioning something about your being in marital discord, perhaps even to the point of a breakup. Is that right?" She hemmed and hawed a little but then agreed that, yes, it was so. She was no longer in love, and the marriage was over, only her husband hadn't yet grasped that fact. He was still around.

"You know," I said, "that's a very stressful situation. It's one of the most stressful situations that a human being can go through, whether or not they are in the throes of awakening."

She said she knew that was true. We then talked about the particulars of her situation, which I'll leave out. What I did as she talked was point out what was apparently true, and question anything that I thought might be inconsistent with other things she'd said. It was not totally unlike the sort investigation we'd undertaken in her initial Awakening Session, and as I probed, a more detailed story began to emerge.

Some years before, prior to the decade she's spent in addiction recovery, Lisa had been diagnosed as being bipolar. That's a common theme among alcoholics. She had been prescribed medication—simple antidepressants. This started a long-running conversation with herself, in her head, as to whether medication was necessary, or beneficial, or if it was somehow stymieing her spiritual quest. The "bad angel" on her shoulder had taken the lead over the "good one" lately, and thus for a while now she had not been fully availing herself of the help those foolish professionals thought she needed: she was off her meds.

Truth sometimes emerges slowly, but given enough encouragement it will typically show itself. Both recovery and Nonduality are at heart cultures of willingness. In those cultures, we are willing to question the status quo over and over again. We are willing to be honest.

Lisa was afraid that medication might give her some kind of false reading, that it might make her feel better than she was "really" feeling, or that it might stifle her. One way or the other, she was afraid it would somehow negatively affect her awakening process. And like most bull-headed seekers and alcoholics, she thought she should be able to work through her life's present turbulence all on her own, without benefit of a medication that is only noticed if there is an absence of it. We do what we do.

I get the reluctance; there's a real point to be made there. We don't want to mask things like memories or emotions. When it makes sense, we want to allow them to emerge, bubble to the top, and then with a pop and a ping we're free of that particular baggage; however, in the case of those who are clinically out of balance, to go off meds is no small decision. It can be serious, even deadly serious, and neither patient, nor observer can know in advance what the results of such an experiment might be.

Let me go on record as saying that this teaching is all about seeing and working with the way things are, right this moment, which includes honoring the unit's needs. What I'm interested in is what works, not what might look or sound good.

I can tell you from long experience that many people in Twelve Step fellowships think taking medication for good mental health is a decidedly bad idea. This kind of bias is prevalent throughout our society. It can be found anywhere from a well-meaning friend's kitchen table to a fundamentalist pulpit. Even in our spiritual community, in what we sometimes think of as wide-open all-inclusive Nonduality, this prejudice may arise from a spiritual teacher or a fellow practitioner. It's important that we realize that these people are not typically educated or trained in medicine—or licensed to practice it. Physician, heal thyself.

Acknowledging that we, as human beings, as awakened beings, and as spiritual teachers and practitioners don't have all the answers about anything, much less everything, is simply the open admission of what is already glaringly true. It's one of the reasons I have a disclaimer on this website. I tell people every day, "I don't have any answers for you. All I have is stories and questions." What I know is that I don't know, which puts me one up in the game. I am what I am, but I'm also not what I'm not.

If I have a client who seems to be stepping into the psychological "wild side," I don't hesitate to recommend they see a psychotherapist, psychiatrist, or other professional. Professionals have specialized knowledge and tools that someone who is not in the field does not have. If my client insists on trying to drag me into what I see as conventional therapeutic territory, I will drop them as a client. I've done it before and I'm open to doing it again.

Let me share a couple of personal stories with you concerning mental health and medication—or the lack of it.

Back in 2002, before Betsy and I were married, she was in the fine woodworking field, and her business partner was bipolar. His illness, which may well have granted him the spark of artistic genius, eventually turned their business venture into a personal and financial disaster. Ben was hospitalized.

Upon his release, some of his friends in the construction industry advised him to just "pull himself up by his bootstraps." Ben liked that advice—he didn't want to take medication anyway. A symptom of bipolar disorder appears to be the belief that one doesn't need to take medication to curb it.

Our beliefs, opinions, and positions (BOPs) are constantly tripping us up and holding us down. We have to be willing to either constantly question our thoughts—to live in inquiry—or accept the consequences of going through our lives following one blind pattern after another. To live consciously awake requires both alertness and openness.

Ben was far from consciously awake. He was suffering mightily, but he didn't want to be thought weak or somehow odd in either his friends' eyes or his own, so one day he quit taking his meds. Again. This time around, however, before an intervention could occur, he put a shotgun in his mouth and blew his head off.

Ben's wife and Betsy both had their lives shattered. Betsy had to declare bankruptcy. I helped her shut the company down. Clients and creditors were stung. Workers were let go. A whole community mourned the death of this gifted artist—enough so that we all came together ten years later to celebrate what he'd meant to us. He was literally BOPped to death.

It is amazing to me that we are still in the dark ages about mental health. A great many of us have all kinds of chemical imbalances. Diabetics have a chemical imbalance, but I don't notice anyone stigmatizing them or coaching them off their meds. Just about everything that can go wrong with human beings is treated chemically: from high blood pressure to heart disease to high cholesterol. All of these things are treatable conditions. Whether we opt for pharmaceuticals or herbs, we're after simple chemical balance, and achieving that balance with meds is both accepted and encouraged in physical illness. Why is mental health the exception? We just can't seem to grow up on this subject; we are inherently suspicious and distrustful of any problem involving the organ we call our brain.

So, in an effort to calm her fears about medication interfering with her clearing process, I shared something with Lisa that I had written about over two years before. "Lisa," I said, "years ago, back when the drinking had gotten very heavy, and my life management skills were shot to hell, I was diagnosed as being bipolar. I take meds, too." Her jaw dropped.

It's well known that I had two stays in a mental hospital in the early 80's. "We don't treat alcoholism here," they said. "Our diagnosis is that you're bipolar." I always thought—because it was what I wanted to think—that I was alcoholic, but not bipolar, and that they were just playing footsie with the rules in order to help me. But the two conditions go hand in glove, and what I see now is that I'm both. I am totally alcoholic, and I seem to have mild case of manic depression.

I don't have big spikes and I don't have deep plunges. We are not talking dark nights of the soul here. That event (which you don't need to have!) took another form entirely. I know what some of you are thinking: who is it that gets depressed? Nobody. Depression arises. And it is experienced without being personalized.

Depression doesn't have any more to do with enlightenment than a nervous tic does. It's a unit-centered condition. Life doesn't get depressed, but the unit can certainly experience it, and if it does, then at the very least it's going to lose a lot of efficiency. In working out what is right for me, I've tried going without medication for several months several times since my initial awakening.

My most recent experiment was about a year ago. Sure enough, there was slow slide that resulted in a loss of energy and a drop in motivation. Betsy noticed a difference and asked me several times if I was okay. I always reported the same thing: "Yes. I am fine, but I do notice that the unit is really tired." Eventually my work began to suffer, even though I, Awakeness, felt the same. That did it. If this teaching was going to be affected, then the experiment was over.

I took Betsy's advice, swallowed my foolish pride and my meds, and then proceeded to write *The Book of Undoing* in three weeks flat. The book was a surprise hit, and with its release my practice immediately began to mushroom. It was a once in a lifetime opportunity, and I'm so grateful that I was ready for it not just spiritually but also psychologically and physically. During sessions with my clients, an energy transfer occurs, and I need to be in decent shape in order to constantly replenish.

I serve best when I serve from balance. I work like a crazy man, and I can use all the help and energy that I can get. That's how I feel today. But I can easily hark back to when I had exactly the same fears that Lisa expressed. Let me answer them here for any of you who are wondering the same things.

Will psychotropic medication prevent you from waking up? No. Will it prevent you from clearing up? No. It's neither the body nor the mind that wakes up. Awakeness itself wakes up. In my experience, Awakeness doesn't hold a negative view about anything, and that would have to include pharmaceuticals. A dream is a dream is a dream. We do what we do until we do something else.

Lisa was even more relieved by my revelation than she was surprised. It simply yanked all the hoodoo out of her mind regarding medication. She's not the first client I've had that conversation with, but she is the most grateful. She immediately began to glow.

When I saw her reaction I knew I'd have to write more about medication and spirituality. As a matter of fact, I've been meaning to address this topic for quite some time, but I notice it keeps being put off. Ego is not gung-ho about this article. For me, that's a golden opportunity to diminish ego further. My rule to that end is to show what you want to hide and hide what you want to show.

Eventually, there's nothing more to hide.

THIRTY-ONE

THE SECRET KEY TO THE MATRIX

I wonder how many of you have seen the Wachowski Brother's classic motion picture, *The Matrix?* If you haven't seen it, check it out. *The Matrix* concerns a computer programmer who learns that what most people experience as reality is actually a virtual reality created by intelligent machines to exploit humanity. Newly freed from this dreamworld, he joins a revolution of others who have also awakened to the truth.

Whether intended or not, it's widely reputed to be a metaphoric representation of how nondual reality—and awakening—could work. If nothing else, it's a terrific science-fiction adventure, and I highly recommend it.

During the last year, I had an Awakening Session with a client who saw something of the *The Matrix* in our work together. He's an engineer, Indian by birth, who lives in California. This is a serious guy, very bright, but with a great sense of humor and the uncanny ability to sum up deep insights about five seconds after he's witnessed them. It happened over and over in the session. I would lead him, he would follow, he'd see the lesson, and then he'd restate the whole experience in a sentence or two.

It was quite remarkable. There were several places where he disagreed with me or simply failed to buy my presentation of Truth. At those junctures I would back up and guide him through it a second time. He'd inevitably see the error in his thinking and immediately acquiesce without the slightest resistance. He was more interested in being free than he was in being right. It's a shining example of that rarest of commodities —genuine humility. Oh, if I could only clone him!

Once my friend saw a thing, he saw all of it. That's when he would restate the insight, partially I think for him to absorb it better, and partially to test his understanding in front of me. He was always willing to be corrected if it meant that it would bolster his growing understanding. But I never had to correct even one of his restatements. In fact, he used some descriptive lines along the way that I immediately promised to steal, but sadly I've forgotten most of them.

One, however, really struck a chord. When we were done, and he was brightly, clearly, beautifully awake, he said, "My God, you've discovered the secret key to the Matrix!" As soon as he said it, I knew he was right. For the first time ever, I knew what was going on here, what I was doing, why it worked, and why it is so different from everything else.

That's essentially what The Living Method is—a special key that opens a back door into the workings of Reality. And although it is centered around coming to know our sacred True Nature, the method itself is not a spiritual method. It's just a key, a thing, like a living skeleton key. I'm in awe of it, but I don't feel like I need to burn incense, or put on a funny hat, or take on a new name in order to use it. It's a wonderful tool. It makes more sense to me now why a guy who has been such a poor example of skillful living (me) ended up with it.

Why not?

It's a odd Truth, but I've discovered that Reality can be talked about virtually forever without necessarily fostering a breakthrough. Articles, books and videos can be helpful, and they even work sometimes. Satsang and retreat sometimes work. Having a near-death experience can work. Or we can be visited by Grace and just "get it" out of the blue. But none of those things are reliable. None of those things are consistent
.

My Indian friend and I spent some time talking not just about awakening and Reality, but about The Living Method itself. Every once in while I get a client who's completely taken with it and wants to talk about its potential ramifications. It has the potential to turn everything on its head. I'm not saying it will, but I'm saying it could. I haven't the slightest idea about what will happen, or God forbid, what "should" happen! But I'm not blind to possibilities.

For some reason, this metaphor of The Living Method as a key to the Matrix really cemented things for me. It took the remaining spiritual hoodoo out of it, and made it acceptably ordinary. It's extraordinarily ordinary, I grant you that, but it really helped free me of the uncomfortable concept of myself as "spiritual teacher," although I'll continue to use that convenient phrase in the name of linguistic efficiency. I don't have to throw the baby out with the bath water.

But it's changed how I see things. The Living Method is a do thing, not a believe-in thing.

My engineer friend is typical of many of us. He's been around quite a while. He's read a lot of books. He lives in the Bay Area, so a lot of high-powered spiritual teachers are local to him, and he's availed himself of them by attending satsang with a couple of famous figures. He already had a head full of Nonduality when we met today. He had a lot of answers, but he was still seeking.

We know, we know, we know. But what's our EXPERIENCE? Who really cares what another person does or does not know or thinks they know? It's the one who knows who is in the way. I don't know very much. I don't have a lot of answers. But I have an endless number of wonderful questions. You've probably heard the old adage that "We come to spirituality to answer our questions, but we begin to make real progress once we start questioning our answers." I'm in full agreement with that. Let us undo. Let us unknow.

I'm not a high-powered spiritual teacher. I'm just a lucky stiff who, like Bilbo Baggins in *The Hobbit*, stupidly got himself into an awful jam and then stumbled upon a magic ring, or in my case, a secret key. Yes, I studied and practiced for a long time prior to awakening, and I was awake for quite a while before hitting on The Living Method, and I study daily even now in an attempt to honor this thing and to be the best teacher I can be. But I don't know how much of that study and practice was or is truly helpful or necessary. I just did what I did and do what I do—I have no idea why!

Never fool yourself: Truth is hiding in plain sight. It's just your view that's skewed, nothing more

You do NOT need to have a showy spiritual experience in order to wake up, and I'd count you as blessed if you didn't have one. They are more trouble after the fact than they are enjoyable during the event.

There is nothing but Truth. Where once I couldn't find it at all, now I can't find anything else. I meet people who are willing to look at it and people who are not. There are people who really want to wake up, and there are people who really want to talk about waking up. I'm fine with both, but I don't like working with the latter.

Regardless, everyone I meet already is It, whether they choose to notice it or would rather pretend to be one of the Wise Monkeys. I wish you luck. And I send you love, because I have nothing else to offer you, except maybe the key to the Matrix.

THIRTY-TWO

TOWARD ABIDANCE AND EMBODIMENT

I want to talk to you today about the real spiritual journey, about the one that truly matters. Awakening doesn't work the way many of us think it does.

I help people wake up nearly every day, and because of that I've learned a great deal about the awakening event and the post-awakening process, as well as the mindset and motivations of both those who seek, and those who find. Regardless of what we might hear to the contrary, my own day-after-day-in-the-trenches experience is that coming to recognize our True Nature is simply not that difficult—not anymore. If it was, I'd still be selling books for a living.

So it's not the allowing ourselves to see our True Nature that's the big bear. The real trouble lies in accepting it. It's not the breakthrough, it's the follow through! Part of the responsibility for this lies in the typical seeker's mindset— the very mindset that I had as a seeker. One of the common themes I discover in both helping people to awaken, and in helping them to stabilize, is the erroneous sense that somehow "our" awakening is about us, for us—individual units. That's what I thought prior to awakening, and it's what I thought when I was on the wrong side of identification afterward—what we often refer to as "oscillation."

Fredness was in quite a bad life situation when awakening occurred, and had been for about 2 1/2 years. My first motivation to wake up was relief. I wanted out of my suffering. That's the most common motivation I find in the field, and there's absolutely nothing wrong with it. My secondary motivation, however, was entirely egoic. Even my notions of somehow being able to help others was egoic. Those I helped would then see how special I was. Enlightenment was something that I wanted to add to the Fred Story.

There's actually nothing inherently awful about this shallow motivation either, simply because whatever it is that brings us to awakening is just fine! If I save a bunch of children because I want my picture in the newspaper, who cares? It's the saving of the children that matters. In this same way, it's the awakening event that's most important, not the mental path we took to arrive at it. There's plenty of opportunity to "go deep" after we awaken by hook or by crook!

But this sort of motivation begins to be a problem if it's carried over into the post-awakening process. The primary early understanding that most of us come to upon an awakening is that we see through the illusion of a separate self. Oneness is "seen," meaning that we experience ourselves as Oneness to one degree or another. It may come with a "bang," or it may come with a barely noticeable "pop" or with no pop at all. It may be seen deeply or barely. We may have context for it or we may not.

Ultimately none of that matters. It's the shift itself that is most important, for once Truth is seen it cannot be totally forgotten. I had a glimpse haunt me for twelve years before I came to a larger, more thorough awakening, but it was that glimpse that allowed me to drive my first stake into a beachhead in Reality and drove me back first to Zen, and then ultimately into a less structured brand of Nonduality. So it is beyond logic—only Maya could pull a stunt like this off—that after awakening, in almost every case, it is the non-existent individual who claims the awakening! "I did it, and it was all about me."

There is a yang for every yin, so when cloudiness again develops—as it almost certainly will—we want to know where "our personal" enlightenment has gotten off to. I spent three years moving between bliss and hell. The more time you spend as Awakeness, the less enchanting—or even pleasant—the dream becomes. And of course I knew that I should be experiencing bliss and clarity in every moment of every day. I knew that awakening was all about living in a constantly enthralled, orgasmic experience. Right? Right?

Wrong.

Yes, that's what I knew, but since that's not the truth, what I knew pitted "me"—the very same nonexistent "me" that had been seen through in the awakening(s)—against Reality, and time and time again I came up the loser. My experience "should be" other than what it is: that is the fundamental dynamic of the dream. And so long as we believe that post-awakening is about the unit and not Awakeness itself, we're going to dream long and lousy.

The first thing we notice when we see things as they really are—when we come to the stark simplicity of What Is—is that What Is is all there is! There is no alternative to exactly what's going on right now—until there is. When that "until there is" arises, it will be as the new face of What Is, not as an alternative. It's one scene at a time, folks. And whatever scene is arising, is the only scene there is until it isn't. And then there's no going back, which would be like trying to hang onto one frame of a movie. Can't be done.

Once we develop enough insight—we could often label that a budding of humility—the true Truth is seen: "our" awakening is not about the ego, and it's not about the unit. That's not to say there are no benefits for the unit! There's no benefit for ego in an awakening—far from it—but there are huge benefits for the unit! My life and Betsy's life are totally different than they used to be, and totally better. The formerly careening human roller coaster of the "thrill of victory, and the agony of defeat" is now still. We still have great interest and take great pleasure in living, and these units maintain some light preferences, but the old, everyday life-and-death intensity of even the smallest matters is simply gone.

When we wake up, meaning when Awakeness suddenly recognizes that it's always already awake, that conscious awareness will be seen to be coming through a particular unit which heretofore only experienced unconscious awakeness. That's what it will look like from the outside. From Awakeness's view, however, all that will be seen is that there is nothing but awakeness, which is sometimes conscious and sometimes unconscious; sometimes cloudy and sometimes clear. And that experience of cloudiness or clarity includes all units, but it's not about them.

The unit, in effect, becomes a window. We have a leg in each world—one in the dream, and one in That which is beyond the dream. This, of course, is language, so it is clumsy and suggests duality. I don't mean that at all. That's why I said in that last sentence "in effect," meaning that I have come as close as I can get with words. That will be the experience. And what awakening is truly all about is allowing That which is beyond the dream to "stream through" unencumbered into the dream by way of skillful action through the surrendered unit.

It's not "our" awakening; it's Awakeness's awakening. The separate personality doesn't wake up to the truth of God; God wakes up to the fiction of the separate personality. There is Fredness—identifiable patterns—but there is no Fred. Or you either. And since there is no separate individual, awakening cannot possibly be about a separate individual, whether that be the experienced "me" or the experienced "you."

We have a skewed perception, and awakening merely straightens that out. Nothing new has to happen; something ancient must be noticed. That's all. If there is an accompanying spiritual experience, the unit is welcome to enjoy it. Have at it! Who doesn't love a spiritual? There is nothing cooler. But none of that has anything to do with enlightenment. Zero.

Awakening doesn't add to us, it strips us down. It's just not about a buzz, or an achievement for these units. It's not self-improvement, it's about Self-recognition on an ongoing basis. It's about the willingness of the apparent personality to be colonized by Awakeness so that it can, at least apparently, shine brighter and broader. It comes to know itself, and to love itself, and that Love then shows up more and more in the world.

That's what it's all about.

Let us be willing to surrender to the face of the present arising. This single moment is all we ever have to surrender to. There is only Now. And that Now is You.

THIRTY-THREE

THE LOOKING GLASS LANGUAGE AS MIRROR

When I wrote this piece early in the spring of 2013. I intentionally sat down to write my best, highest, clearest piece ever.

The Looking Glass: Language As Mirror was the first post I wrote after deciding I would no longer host other teachers, but write everything myself instead. I wanted to try to bring attention to The Living Method of Awakening, which had been steadily developing itself for almost a year. I wanted something that would really make a mark—at least on me, and hopefully beyond my neighborhood.

Funny things can happen when you really commit yourself to a spiritual project. Right now as I write this introduction it is 6:30 a.m. I am not an early riser; it's been an all-nighter as I've put the finishing touches on this book. I'm usually a bit of a night-owl, but I haven't stayed up all night for many, many years.

134

When It takes you, it does what it does with you until it lets you go. You can go quietly, or you can leave claw marks, but you're going. I got a lot of help the day that I wrote this. I knew what was coming through my pen wasn't coming from my head. must have done something right, because site traffic instantly took off like a rocket. And kept growing and growing and growing...

In short, The Looking Glass is the most popular piece I've ever published, and the reception it got rocked my world. Tens of thousands of people from all over the globe came to read it, and re-read it. People sent links to friends and groups. Others hung links all over the Nondual web. It became an event.

I suddenly began to get emails from people who had woken up from reading this post. Session bookings spiked as I worked with people who had woken up from it, but wanted a deeper seeing, or with people who'd had the ground shift, but needed a little more help. Gratitude letters poured into my inbox.

Pop, pop, pop! The Looking Glass started a small epidemic of awakenings!

I slept very, very little in March of 2013. I did Skype sessions and sold books by day, and wrote The Book of Undoing by night. I had some momentum, and I wanted to utilize it before it subsided. I basically put an Awakening Session into print—at least as they happened at that time.

The Book of Undoing went from initial-idea to available-to-purchase in three weeks flat. I'm a fast typist, but for that three weeks I simply could not write fast enough. The words tumbled from my head and onto the screen in a torrent. I had friends read it and help me edit it as I went—people steeped in authentic spirituality—and all of them were absolutely crazy for it.

Just as I knew I was writing something different, so they knew they were reading something different. Something fresh had come into the world, and it was singing the song of Truth.

No one was more surprised than I was when the book became an instant hit, climbing onto Amazon's Top Ten Bestsellers for Eastern Philosophy the day after it came out. It stayed there for the next ten months, selling thousands of copies. As a result, people from six continents tried The Living Method of Awakening for themselves, and found that it lived up to its billing.

It worked.

What a mad, mad, amazing year it was during that first year! So much has happened that it feels like a decade has passed. This post, this almost poem-like thing, this whatever-it-is started it all. I slipped The Looking Glass into the back of The Book of Undoing, because I wanted it in print. I'm slipping it in The Book of Unknowing, because I want you to read it.

The Looking Glass has changed a lot of lives, mine chief among them. I wish you ever- increasing clarity as it takes you into its spell.

Good luck!

The Looking Glass

Language as Mirror

Notice that you're already awake.

Right now, this moment, the only reason you can read these words is that you're awake. You're *already* awake. You're as awake as it gets. You're already *fully* awake.

Given that you're already fully awake, how then could you wake up *further?* Since you're already awake, does that idea even make sense? You can't wake up *more* from where you are right now. And certainly you can't wake up *again.*

If you want to read a book through that body you're wearing, or watch a video, or send it to a retreat for further clarity or to get some context that has the potential to open the door to further clarity, that's great. But before you do, notice that you don't *need* to read another book, watch a video, or go to a retreat in order to wake up, because you're already awake.

If you want to do meditation, drum, dance, chant, or what have you, for the sake of grounding yourself in that present human experience you're having, or calming that unit's mind so that you can better hear yourself talk to yourself, and better watch yourself dance for yourself, terrific. Have at it. But, be absolutely aware that you can't practice yourself into awakening. You can't *achieve* what you *already are.*

You're just not who you think you are; that's the only issue here. You're undergoing a case of mistaken identity, and all you need today is a little light reflected from this mirror, this mirror of clear language that is *also* you. There is *only* you, but you tend to get a bit cloudy sometimes, and forget that. It comes with the territory when your spaciousness apparently contracts around apparent human beings, and it's no big deal. It's fine. When you're ready to be clear you find a bright mirror, so here you are, back in front of the vanity mirror that is *also* you!

Vanity, vanity, all is vanity! This is *all* you, every bit of it--you dancing for you, you preening for you, just you showing off *for* yourself, *to* yourself and loving it--loving this loving yourself.

You think you're the human being reading these words.

You're not. Well, you actually *are that human also,* but you're not that person *exclusively.* You're the awareness that's reading these words *through* that human being. The human is not reading the words; *you* are. The human is a reading tool for you just as reading glasses are a tool for the human. Reading glasses never mistake themselves for being the reader; humans almost always do.

You think you need to wake up. You don't. All that has to occur is for you to recognize yourself as what you truly are. "Awaken" makes it sound like something special, and new, and different needs to happen. It doesn't. *Recognition,* on the other hand, is simply about noticing what already is. See how much lighter the idea of recognition is versus the idea of waking up? Why make it hard on yourself, when you're clearly longing to see/be your true nature again?

Why not do this the easy way? Be gentle to yourself. How much effort does it take for that human to recognize itself in a mirror? None. The same is true for you. You just have to be willing to look in the mirror and see the *reflection* instead of the *projection.*

Stop seeking outwardly for just a few minutes. After all, you have all the time in the world! Reverse your attention. Take your plain old attention, what feels like your *personal* attention, and turn it around. Look *back* instead of *out.*

Notice how easy it is to move your attention whenever and wherever you want to move it. Notice how whatever attention finds tends to *expand.* See how easy it is for you to pull *globalized* awareness, meaning the background, unfocused awareness that is always running, and reform it into *localized* awareness.

Notice how once you've seen what you wanted to see, the apparent localization drops of its own accord, once again leaving boundless globalized awareness in its stead. It just *happens;* you don't have to do a thing. All of this is working *for* you. It's always here, always running, and certainly it's always awake. It has to be. It's all *part* of you, part of the one thing going on--*you.*

You have always been awake, always will be, *cannot fail* to be awake. Awakeness is not a *trait* of yours, it's what you actually *are.*

Back to the attention exercise. What do you see when you turn back and look for yourself? What do you find? Can you actually find yourself? Check. Really look.

Do you find any*thing*?

Any*one?* No, you can't find yourself, because there's nothing objective there to see. There's a sense of *something* being there, but there's nothing locatable, because there's nothing objective. But clearly there *is* something there, and it's absolutely *alive.* You can feel that, can you not? Isn't there almost a *stirring,* perhaps a *tingling,* a certain *presence,* perhaps behind your eyes, in your chest, or around your head? It's undefinable, but it's there. Always. You can feel it if you let yourself. *Let yourself.*

The we-who-are-you have a *word,* a sort of *name* for that undefinable, living presence you discover when you look back and try to find yourself and can't. We can't call it *something,* but neither is it *nothing,* hence we have arrived at *no-thing.*

This no-thing, this pure subjectivity, this keen awareness that's looking out through the eyes of that human you're wearing is what you are. You have been on an endless search for something unfindable. It ends when you end it, and not before.

In Nondual teachings it is said, "The eye can't see itself." They mean that *you* are that invisible eye. You can't see yourself when you look back, because *you're the no-thing doing the looking.* Let that hit you. Let that settle in. *Feel it.* Right there, that bit of a line, is the wide open Gateless Gate, enlightenment in a nutshell. What you've been looking *with*--your magical *attention,* which is nothing more than focused awareness--is what you've been looking *for*--unfocused awareness which is the living background of all things. You've been a dog chasing its tail. You can chase it for an entire lifetime, and never find it so long as you continue to look outward, which is where your attention is naturally drawn. Such is the fate of most seekers. You don't have to be one of them.

You can't *see* yourself, you can't really *find* yourself, but you can *sense* yourself. You can *know* yourself. Right now! In fact, you can't know anything else! And you'll never know yourself *later*. There *is* *no* later. So *notice yourself*--know yourself right now! Pay attention to attention!

Notice that I didn't have to say, *"Wake up* and look for yourself." You are always already awake, and you are always already here. Ever since you started this so-called spiritual journey, you've been looking for "some other level" of awakeness. Listen to me closely. *There is no other level of awakeness.* This *everyday* awakeness that you've experienced every day of your life is the *very same* awareness that all the saints and sages have talked about since time immemorial. There is only the *single* awareness, only Not-two! *You are that very awareness.* At every step on your so-called spiritual path you've been looking for "some other kind" of awareness. Hear me. *There is no other kind of awareness.*

It *feels like* that human body contains consciousness, that it is the holder of the most precious thing--"your" awareness.

It doesn't. It can't! A human can't hold you! Nothing can hold you! You hold everything! You are the aware space that everything appears in. THIS aware space! The ONLY aware space there is! You permeate all humans, every single one of them, inside and out. You've hitherto thought that there actually is something called "your consciousness." There isn't. Pay close attention.

You *are* "your consciousness," and you are simultaneously *everyone's* "personal consciousness." I say this lightly, almost laughingly, because *there is no personal consciousness.* Consciousness is not something you *have,* it's what you *are.* Nothing can take that from you, not even death. When that human body dies, you just change channels. Your focused attention goes elsewhere within your unfocused awareness. There's nowhere else to go. You dial up another dream. It's always Movie Night for you!

Let's look at the notion that awareness, or consciousness, is something you *have.* It's quite a convincing story that you have set up for yourself there.

Shut those eyes for a minute. If you're interested in having that long-sought-after spiritual awakening that that particular human has been going on and on about for damn near *forever,* that it's driven itself *crazy* over, then don't just *read* this: *do it.* Read this all the way through, then close those eyes, relax that body, and go through the exercise.

Notice that without benefit of sight you can still tell that you're alive.

You still know that *you are,* sight or no sight. Imagine you're in utter silence. Wouldn't you still know you were alive in the absence of sound? Wouldn't you still be able to sense the usually subtle *pulsing of aliveness* within the body? Of course you would. You would *know.* If we stuffed cotton in those ears, wouldn't you still know that you were there--or rather that *you are here?* So, without benefit of either sight or hearing you can still tell that you're alive. The knowledge that you are is not dependent on certain conditions or tools. You *cannot fail* to know that you are.

In fact, if I took that unit you're wearing and dropped it into a sensory deprivation chamber, you would *still* know that you're alive. That knowing is not dependent on sensations, perceptions, thoughts, memories, or any other *information.* It's not dependent on *anything.* In fact, everything is dependent on *it!* That knowing is *primary.* It's the only thing for which there is no opposite.

Can you imagine not knowing yourself?

No, you cannot. That knowing *has no opposite,* thus it's unimaginable. It "cannot not" be! Knowing would have to be present in order to report that it doesn't know itself! The question collapses.

That knowing is the One True No-thing.

But that knowing is really knowing*ness,* is it not? You are not a *static* knowing. You are not some kind of grand *noun.* You are beyond noun-ness. And all these years you've been looking for some kind of vague, but grand *object* so that you could *experience* yourself. *You cannot experience what you are.*

You are beyond verbness too; however, verbness, in a display that is constantly shifting, morphing, changing from one extreme to the other and back again; evolving and devolving, forward and back, is always arising *to you,* to that-which-does-not-move-but-is-not-static. *You arise to yourself.* We-who-are-also-you vaguely call that verbness "the world," which expands or contracts to suit your purposes. It might be a thought, a sound, a room, or it might be a whole universe. Regardless, *whatever arises is not other than you.*

You are what you know, and what you know, you are.

The seeker is the sought.

Notice that knowingness. Stop and notice it *now.* Become conscious of it, hold it within attention--*be* the attention--so that you can come to recognize it clearly. Feel it. In the absence of that knowingness, there is no world. In the presence of that knowingness the world arises, fully formed. You don't have to do a thing; it just *happens.*

Notice that the knowing doesn't need to wake up, in fact *cannot* wake up, because it's always already awake. See that it's the knowingness that's come to know itself. We call this knowingness-knowing-itself *conscious awareness,* versus unconscious awareness, which is still awake and alive and aware, but not consciously. Either way it's still you. One way you're cloudy, one way you're clear, but there's just one thing going on, and that one thing is *you.*

You are *already* Home. You have *always* been Home. There is nothing *other than* Home.

If you are already Home, how would you ever find it by looking for it? You'd always be looking away from it. You find Home only when you notice it's where you already are, always have been, and always will be, because there is nothing other than Home. There is nothing other than *This.* Look!

I'm talking about THIS This! THIS very This where you already are! We don't find Home by *going after it;* we find it by *stopping within it.* Any directions on how to *get* Home are by definition directions leading *away* from home. But they are great for tiring you out! And it's all good fun--until it's not.

Take a quick inventory.

What have you been using all these years in your search for enlightenment? *Awareness.* What has been reading all the books? *Awareness.* What has been watching all the videos, and listening to the teachers? *Awareness.* If you meditate, what is it that watches your breath, or your thoughts, or counts, or tries to let go of doing all that, or gets annoyed because you can't adequately escape the nagging now in order to enjoy some other experience *that would, of course, arise and fall within the nagging now?* It's *Awareness.* What is it that prays? *Awareness.* What is it that asks, "Who am I?" until it wants to scream? *Awareness.*

Awareness has been in a millennia-long search *for* awareness. It's been looking for *some other* awareness. Hear me: *there is no other awareness.*

This is it. THIS This is all there is.

Oneness cannot find otherness no matter how long or hard it looks, because *there is no otherness* for oneness to find. The definition of oneness

141

could be said to be *no-other-to-find*. If you're searching for some other, as you have been, and there IS no other, how long can you look? If all is oneness, where do you imagine you're standing while you're looking for the oneness? In the   oneness!

Always! Forever!

So long as you insist on looking forward, so long as you are seeking something outside yourself, you'll never find yourself, never hook up with yourself, never ever "awaken," at least not in *this* life. So for goodness sakes, *stop.*

Why continue in this compulsive looking for something that's totally unfindable? You've been hot on the trail of a *phantom.* STOP!

Once you *sense* what you are, once you take that giant leap to the *utterly obvious* and recognize what you are--*that which is looking*--there may or may not be a sharp sense of realization.

It doesn't matter. All of that bliss and fireworks, fun as it might be, is candy. It's completely unnecessary--it has nothing to do with awakening any more than a car has to do with the driver's body. It's simply a *vehicle,* and just like cars, and planes and trains, there are all kinds of vehicles, none inherently more important than the other. It's about the damn *trip,* not the vehicle! Any bells and whistles are just bells and whistles. They're just pleasant distractions.

What matters is simple *recognition,* because however you display yourself to yourself, you're almost surely going to have to come back to *fresh* conscious recognition over and over again. This is the discipline part. This is the process part. This is where you use that unit to help you. Don't try to transcend the unit--*use it!* Just because that unit uses a shovel to dig a hole, it doesn't think it's the shovel. That unit is a tool. *Deign to use it.*

All of the ramifications of the seeing/being What Is are not immediately obvious. They will fill in as your understanding increases. You see what you need to see when you need to see it, not before. Work with what you have and more will come. That's how it works. We are like spies; we work on a need-to-know basis.

You may tell yourself, "It can't be that simple." *It is.* Recognition starts with seeing the seer--or rather, *not* seeing the seer! No seer, no seen, only *seeing.* Only an object can see, only an object can be seen, and you, of course, are not an object. All objects appear *within* you, arise *to* you. You are what is primary. There may be lots of other *relatively real* stuff, a whole world full of it, but you are the One True No-thing.

This seeing is so amazing that you may want to claim it. But *who will it be* that wants to claim it? That unit cannot hold such seeing in its head, cannot store it up for later recall. Only *you* can behold *you*--and then only *right now*.

Liberation is all about right now, *this* moment. Are you consciously awake to *this* current arising? Yesterday's seeing is yesterday's dust. Other than being a gnawing reminder, it has no present value whatsoever. Freedom is now or never, here or nowhere.

This simple recognition of your true nature is not the end of your apparent journey, but it can be the end of all this compulsive seeking you've been doing--if you let it.

It can be the most important step you *never take*. Just STOP.

Look at what's looking. Pay attention to attention.

You can *overcome* this simple seeing if you want to--99% of humans do. They do it all the time. This is why everyone wants a big, splashy spiritual experience. They think if they have a flashy experience, *an S&M-style spiritual experience where they will be tied up and made to see the truth*, they will not then be able to overcome it with incessant thinking. That's not true. People do it all the time anyway. They think that just because they got a big, lazy peek at things that they can stay awake and lazy at the same time. They can't. They sit on their haunches, and they get cloudier and cloudier. And that's fine, too. But it certainly can't be labeled skillful.

You don't ever go to sleep, but you can most certainly delude yourself and *appear* to go to sleep. It's what you do--in almost every single one of these human suits you're wearing.

You are always awake, but you are not always *consciously* awake. In fact, you are *rarely* consciously awake. And because you've been unconsciously awake for thousands of years in that *package*--meaning the DNA and softer conditioning associated with the body you thought you were when you first started reading this--you'll fall right back into unconsciousness if you don't consistently and actively *nourish it* with conscious light.

You have to be willing to shine truth, even when you don't feel like yourself, even when you don't want to, on things you'd rather leave in the dark. You must hold nothing back. Willingness is your bridge into *being the shining* on an ongoing basis. You give yourself to the light *fully,* or you don't give yourself at all.

Don't bother trying to figure any of this out, or you'll end up right back on the same hamster wheel from which you just hopped off. You don't have to figure anything out.

Let the mind live in uncertainty. Let the body do what it does.

You do what *you* do: just watch, just be alert. You are not the watcher, you are the *watching,* you are the light behind alertness.

But when you're watching as *conscious* awareness instead of *unconscious* awareness, then what you see will change. Look at any human life and you'll see lots and lots of hopeless, blind patterns, compulsive energy patterns that are just running by themselves, with no one at the wheel, and no good end in sight. Once they were successful, now they're not, yet still they run. And run and run and run.

You'll see a long trail of unskillful living, a long trail of suffering. If you're willing to really look at the patterns, they will start to change.

These patterns are very specific, so *each one* has to be shined on by the light of your conscious awareness in order for it to be remedied; in order for there to be clearing. Awareness colonizes the body one bit, one seeing, one unconscious pattern at a time.

Don't try to fix that unit.

You can't anyway; that body is operating on its own. You are not its minder or controller. It's doing what it does until it does something else. *Let it*--it will do so, regardless. It won't do something else until it sees that what it's already doing isn't helpful, isn't skillful, isn't beneficial to the well being of the unit and the world. But once it *does* see that, once it truly and thoroughly sees it, then that *penetrated pattern* will thin, recede, drop away of its own accord. You don't have to do a thing. It just *happens.* Clarity arises. It may happen quickly, or it may happen slowly, but once an unskillful pattern has been fully penetrated, its days are numbered.

This process of bringing light to all of your dark corners is what we call *embodiment.* Slowly, sometimes excruciatingly slowly, you will begin to "live up to your seeing," so to speak. There's no rush. When you're done with that body, you have seven billion more to turn to, and that's just on *this* planet!

Your willingness to be consciously awake to *this* present arising--is critical. Will you stand as awareness and see things as they are, or stand as a hypothetical center of consciousness, and wish for what isn't? In every moment you ally yourself either with experience, or thinking. You have a history of voting for thinking. It'll take some work to shift that default position. It'll take a *lot* of willingness.

This willingness must extend *all the way down.* Even when you revert to feeling like you are that human character again, as you almost surely will, you have to be willing to take that character's thinking into inquiry. You have to be willing to remain forever open to doubt, to embrace uncertainty. Sureness will be a thing of the past, but living in the mysterious unfolding of yourself is *so much* more satisfying.

Ask yourself again and again, "Is what I'm thinking really true, or is it a belief, an opinion, a position? A BOP?"

Again and again, as you *touch* truth through actual experience--as you *discover* truth through continuous inquiry--that touch will bring a longer, stronger, more profound experience of what you always already are--that which *knows* that you are.

Eventually, the inquiry becomes less formal and more spontaneous. You won't always have to take your thoughts about arisings through a process of formal inquiry. Life itself becomes constant inquiry. Delusion arises, it's questioned, penetrated, and it drops. Pop, pop, pop. Like everything else, you don't have to do a thing. It just happens effortlessly. It's all for *you.*

We-who-are-also-you call this effortless living *abiding.* We call it *abiding enlightenment,* because you are then consciously living in the awakeness that you know yourself to be, and operating within the world *as* that awakeness.

Did this nudge you out of cloudiness, and back toward clarity? If it did, be willing to read it again. If it worked at all for you the first time, it'll permeate deeper as you reread it. *Repetition is the mother of clarity.* Be well. Be *wellness.*

~The Beginning~